TEMPOS VERBAIS em INGLÊS

Verb Tenses

Elisabeth Prescher

TEMPOS VERBAIS em INGLÊS

Verb Tenses

5ª reimpressão

DISAL EDITORA

© 2011 Elisabeth Prescher

Revisão
Carla Finger

Capa e projeto gráfico
Paula Astiz

Editoração eletrônica
Laura Lotufo / Paula Astiz Design

Assistente editorial
Aline Naomi Sassaki

Dados Internacionais de Catalogação na Publicação (CIP)
(Câmara Brasileira do Livro, SP, Brasil)

Prescher, Elisabeth
　　Tempos verbais em inglês : verb tenses/Elisabeth Prescher. — Barueri, SP : DISAL, 2011.

　　ISBN 978-85-7844-069-5

　　1. Inglês - Verbos - Tempos I. Título.

11-00515　　　　　　　　　　　　　　　　　　CDD-425

Índices para catálogo sistemático:
1. Tempos verbais : Inglês : Linguística　425
2. Verbos : Tempos : Inglês : Linguística　425

DISAL EDITORA

Todos os direitos reservados em nome de:
Bantim, Canato e Guazzelli Editora Ltda.

Alameda Mamoré 911 – cj. 107
Alphaville – BARUERI – SP
CEP: 06454-040
Tel./Fax: (11) 4195-2811
Visite nosso site: www.disaleditora.com.br
Televendas: (11) 3226-3111

Fax gratuito: 0800 7707 105/106
E-mail para pedidos: comercial@disal.com.br

Nenhuma parte desta publicação pode ser reproduzida, arquivada ou transmitida de nenhuma forma ou meio sem permissão expressa e por escrito da Editora.

Sumário

Introdução

definindo
    tempo, verbo comum e auxiliar   7
    verbo regular, irregular, particípio e gerúndio   8
    tempos verbais   9
    auxiliares e auxiliares modais   10

auxiliares
    be, have, do   12

modais
    can, could, may, might, must, will, shall, would, should   15

Tempos verbais

visão geral, verbos raramente usados em progressive tenses   21

simple tenses
    simple present   25
    simple past   31
    simple future   39

progressive tenses
    present progressive   43
    past progressive   49
    future progressive   53

perfect tenses
    present perfect   57
    past perfect   63
    future perfect   67

perfect progressive tenses
    present, past, future   71

conditional tenses
    simple, progressive, perfect, perfect progressive   75

Apêndice

1   Formas verbais abreviadas   83

2   Grafia: final s/es, d/ed, ing   85

3   Tempos Verbais x Voz Passiva   87

4   Modos   89

5   Prática adicional   91

6   Respostas dos exercícios   99

7   Lista de verbos irregulares   113

Introdução

Antes do estudo específico dos Tempos Verbais (Verb Tenses) em Inglês, apresentamos ao leitor as ferramentas necessárias para a construção e compreensão deles. Tais ferramentas incluem noções de tempo (tense), distinção entre verbo comum, auxiliar e modal, verbos regulares e irregulares, particípio passado e particípio presente etc. Os termos e elementos apresentados nesta introdução serão os que o leitor irá encontrar ao longo do livro.

TEMPO

Tempo (tense) é uma categoria gramatical que situa a ação no tempo, ou seja, indica quando a ação acontece.

Apenas dois tempos (tenses) são formados pelo verbo sozinho: o simple present (como em 'I work') e o simple past (como em 'I worked'). Os demais tempos são formados com o auxílio de outros verbos, os chamados 'auxiliares' (como em 'I am working').

VERBOS COMUNS E AUXILIARES

Em inglês, os verbos podem ser classificados como comuns (ordinary) e auxiliares (auxiliaries). A maioria dos verbos é 'comum' como: **work**, **talk**, **eat**, **live** etc. De maneira geral, os verbos comuns têm:

uma forma base	*write*	*talk*
uma forma para o presente	*write/s*	*talk/s*
uma para o passado	*wrote*	*talked*
uma para o particípio passado	*written*	*talked*
uma para o particípio presente	*writing*	*talking*

VERBOS REGULARES E IRREGULARES

Os verbos comuns podem ser regulares (regular) ou irregulares (irregular). Os regulares seguem determinadas normas para a formação do passado e do particípio passado (verbo + **d/ed**). Os irregulares, ao contrário, variam de forma no passado e no particípio passado.

Observe as seguintes formas de passado:

regular verbs: work – worked   dance – danced   talk – talked
irregular verbs: write – wrote   cut – cut   buy – bought

PARTICÍPIO PASSADO, PARTICÍPIO PRESENTE E GERÚNDIO

O particípio passado (past participle) é usado na formação dos 'perfect tenses' (como em 'I have written').

A terminação do particípio passado dos verbos regulares é igual à do passado (verbo + **d/ed**). Já os verbos irregulares têm formas próprias para o passado e particípio passado. Gramáticas e livros de inglês trazem, em seu final, verbos irregulares, na seguinte ordem: forma base ou infinitivo – passado – particípio passado (lista completa na pág. 113).

Observe:

Base Form	Simple Past	Past Participle
break	broke	broken
catch	caught	caught
cut	cut	cut
go	went	gone
mean	meant	meant

O particípio presente (present participle) e o gerúndio (gerund) são idênticos na forma (verbo + **ing**). A diferença entre eles está no uso.

O particípio presente é usado na formação dos 'progressive' ou 'continuous tenses':

*I am **writing**.*   *He was **working**.*   *They will be **sleeping**.*
(Estou escrevendo.)   (Ele estava trabalhando.)   (Eles estarão dormindo.)

O gerúndio é usado como substantivo, como objeto de preposição ou após determinados verbos:

Reading *is a good pastime.* (A leitura é um bom passatempo.)
*I am tired **of** working.* (Estou cansado de trabalhar.)
*The kids **enjoy** going to school.* (As crianças gostam de ir para a escola.)

TEMPOS VERBAIS (VERB TENSES)

Devido ao uso de auxiliares para a construção da maioria das formas verbais, existe certa polêmica sobre a quantidade exata dos tempos verbais em inglês. Seriam dois – presente e passado? Três – presente, passado e futuro? Quatro, incluindo o condicional? Doze, dezesseis?

Para sermos mais precisos, em Inglês há: dois tempos – 'present' e 'past'; quatro aspectos – 'simple', 'progressive', 'perfect' e 'perfect progressive'; três modos – 'indicative', 'subjunctive' e 'imperative' e duas vozes – 'active' e 'passive'.

Para simplificar o estudo, iremos ignorar parcialmente tais nomenclaturas. Abordaremos 16 itens da voz ativa que chamaremos de 'tenses'– 4 'simple', 4 'perfect' e 8 'progressive' (ou 'continuous'). Os 'conditional tenses', embora fazendo parte deste conjunto, serão estudados em um módulo à parte.

Tenses	Present	Past	Future	Conditional
Simple	I write (escrevo)[1]	I wrote (escrevi)	I will write (escreverei)	I would write (escreveria)
Progressive	I am writing (estou escrevendo)	I was writing (estava escrevendo)	I will be writing (estarei escrevendo)	I would be writing (estaria escrevendo)
Perfect	I have written (tenho escrito)	I had written (tinha escrito)	I will have written (terei escrito)	I would have written (teria escrito)
Perfect Progressive	I have been writing (tenho estado escrevendo)	I had been writing (tinha estado escrevendo)	I will have been writing (terei estado escrevendo)	I would have been writing (teria estado escrevendo)

VERBOS AUXILIARES X AUXILIARES MODAIS (AUXILIARY VERBS X MODAL AUXILIARIES)

Verbos auxiliares ou modais aparecem sempre junto a um verbo comum. De modo geral, eles auxiliam os verbos comuns a expressarem forma ou significado.

Embora os verbos a seguir sejam todos, de alguma forma, verbos auxiliares, convencionou-se chamar simplesmente de auxiliares (auxiliaries) os verbos **be**, **do** e **have** e de auxiliares modais (modal auxiliaries) os verbos **can**, **could**, **may**, **might**, **must**, **shall**, **should**, **will** e **would**.

---

[1] Ver traduções mais adequadas nas páginas de cada tempo verbal.

Os auxiliares podem ajudar um verbo comum a formar negativas e interrogativas *(do)*, a construir tempos contínuos e voz passiva *(be)* ou a construir tempos perfeitos *(have)*:

do – *Do you love me?* (Você me ama?)
I don't like tea. (Não gosto de chá.)

be – *He is studying.* (Ele está estudando.)
The vase was broken. (O vaso foi quebrado.)

have – *They have arrived.* (Eles chegaram.)
He had left. (Eles tinha saído)

Os **auxiliares modais** acrescentam significado aos verbos comuns.

I swim. (Eu nado.)
*I'm upset. I **must** swim.* (Estou aborrecido. Preciso nadar.)

De maneira geral, os verbos auxiliares têm as seguintes formas:

Base Form	Present Tense	Past Tense	Present Participle	Past Participle
be	am, is, are	was, were	being	been
do	do, does	did	doing	done
have	have, has	had	having	had
can (be able to)	can	could	—	—
may (be allowed to)	may	might	—	—
must (have to)	must	—	—	—
will	will	would	—	—
shall	shall	should	—	—

AUXILIARIES BE, DO, HAVE

*He **is walking** to school.*
*They **didn't arrive** early.*
*We **have been** to China many times.*

Os verbos **be** (ser, estar), **do** (fazer) e **have** (ter) são considerados verbos comuns quando usados sozinhos e auxiliares quando junto a outros verbos:

comum: *I **do** my homework.* (Faço minha lição de casa.)
auxiliar: *He **doesn't work** hard.* (Ele não trabalha muito.)

AS FORMAS

a. **afirmativa**

Simple Present

be	**do**	**have**
I **am**	I **do**	I **have**
you **are**	you do	you have
he/she/it **is**	he/she/it **does**	he/she/it **has**
we are	we do	we have
you are	you do	you have
they are	they do	they have

Simple Past

I **was**	I/you/he/she/it/	I/you/he/she/it/
you **were**	we/you/they **did**	we/you/they **had**
he/she/it **was**		
we were		
you were		
they were		

b. **negativa** – acrescenta-se **NOT** ao verbo auxiliar:

*We **were not** sleeping.* *He **does**[2] **not** run fast.* *He **has not** arrived.*
(Não estávamos dormindo.) (Ele não corre rápido.) (Ele não chegou.)

c. **interrogativa** – coloca-se o auxiliar antes do sujeito:

***Were** they sleeping?* ***Did** they work hard?* ***Had**[3] they had lunch?*
(Eles estavam dormindo?) (Eles trabalharam muito?) (Eles tinham almoçado?)

d. **interrogativa-negativa** – coloca-se o verbo auxiliar na forma negativa e abreviada antes do sujeito:

***Aren't** you sleeping?* ***Don't** you love me?* ***Haven't** they arrived?*
(Você não está dormindo?) (Você não me ama?) (Eles não chegaram?)

mas, *Am I **not** late?*
(Não estou atrasado?)

e. **formas abreviadas**

am not — 'm not   do not — don't   have not — haven't
are not — aren't   does not — doesn't   has not — hasn't
is not — isn't   did not — didn't   had not — hadn't
was not — wasn't
were not — weren't

---

2. Quando o auxiliar **do** está presente na frase: (1) não é traduzido e (2) o verbo principal fica na forma base.
3. **Have** como verbo principal: usa o **do** como auxiliar: Do you have cats?

PRACTICE (Respostas na pág. 99)

1. Fill in the blanks with **be** or **have**.

   1. ___Is___ Michael Jackson a singer?
   2. _____ Ronaldo a soccer player?
   3. _____ he your friend?
   4. She _____ two brothers.
   5. _____ they friends?
   6. _____ we on the right road?
   7. I _____ some friends in London.
   8. This _____ a very big house.
   9. We _____ a tennis match on Sunday.
   10. Alex _____ an old car.

2. Answer the questions. Use short answers.

   11. Do you like science fiction?   Yes, __I do_____.
   12. Have you been here before?   Yes, __I have_____.
   13. Are you a student?   No, __I am not_____.
   14. Is skydiving dangerous?   Yes, __it is_____.
   15. Are you writing a letter?   Yes, _____.
   16. Are you going to buy a book?   No, _____.
   17. Have they arrived?   No, _____.
   18. Were the girls late?   Yes, _____.
   19. Does Janice live in Rio?   No, _____.
   20. Was Gary at school yesterday?   No, _____.
   21. Did you understand?   Yes, _____.
   22. Were you angry at me?   Yes, _____.
   23. Are Ann and John your parents?   No, _____.
   24. Did you see them last week?   No, _____.
   25. Does Linda speak Italian?   Yes, _____.

3. Supply the correct form of ***do***, ***be*** or ***have***.

1. *The show _was_ horrible. I _didn't_ like it.*
2. _____ *they live near us?*
3. _____ *you walk home yesterday?*
4. _____ *the kids tired after class?*
5. _____ *John at home when you arrived?*
6. _____ *the girls like apples?*
7. _____ *Paul understand French?*
8. _____ *you seen my brother?*
9. _____ *Kelly worked a lot?*
10. _____ *you happy today?*
11. _____ *your brother at home?*
12. *He* _____ *home, he is at school.*
13. *We* _____ *a house in the country years ago.*
14. _____ *your baby sleep well?*
15. _____ *the boys want to go to the park?*

MODAL AUXILIARIES

*He **can walk** to school.*
*We **should get** home before noon.*

De forma geral, os auxiliares modais acrescentam significado aos demais verbos, atribuindo conceitos como opinião, julgamento, vontade, desejo, possibilidade, probabilidade e obrigação.

Presente	Passado	significado
may	might	possível mas incerto, com permissão, sugerido
can	could	possível, capaz, opcional, com permissão
must	—	necessário, urgente, dedução lógica, proibição
shall	should	futuro provável, futuro pretendido, aconselhável
will	would	futuro definido, prometido, desejado

Os auxiliares modais

1. são sempre seguidos pela forma base de um verbo:
   *I may **go**.* (Posso ir.)
2. não variam de forma:
   *I/They **can** swim.* (Eu posso/Eles podem nadar.)
3. constroem as próprias negativas e interrogativas:
   ***Will** you go?* (Você irá?)
4. não tem todos os tempos (tenses).

Observe:

may/might (pode/podia, poderia)
* pode ser substituído por **be allowed to**
* forma abreviada: —
  May *I leave now?* (Posso sair agora?)
  *You **may not** bring her.* (Você não deve trazê-la.)
  *We **might** visit the zoo.* (Poderíamos visitar o zoológico.)
  *He **was allowed to** leave sooner.* (Ele pôde/Foi-lhe permitido sair mais cedo.)

can/could (pode/podia, poderia)
* pode ser substituído por **be able to**
* formas abreviadas: can not/cannot – can't   could not – couldn't
  ***Can** that baby swim?* (Aquele bebê pode/sabe nadar?)
  *They **could** not help us.* (Eles não puderam nos ajudar.)
  *She **was able to** climb the Everest.* (Ela pôde/conseguiu escalar o Everest.)

must (precisar, ter de)
* pode ser substituído por **have to**
* forma abreviada: must not — mustn't (= proibição)
  *He **must** study hard.* (Ele precisa estudar muito.)
  *You **mustn't** smoke here.* (Você não pode/É proibido fumar aqui.)
  *You **have to** talk to her.* (Você precisa falar com ela.)
  *We **had to** study hard.* (Nós tivemos que estudar muito.)

will/shall

* **will:** usado na formação do 'simple future'.
* **shall:** usado na formação do futuro formal ou pedido polido.
* formas abreviadas: will — 'll   shall — 'll
  will not — won't   shall not — shan't

I **will** talk to her. (Falarei com ela.)
They **will** not follow us. (Eles não vão nos seguir.)
Will she come tonight? (Ela virá esta noite?)
Shall we go now? (Podemos ir agora?)

would/should

* **would:** usado principalmente com orações condicionais.
* **should** (deveria)
* formas abreviadas: would — 'd
  would not — wouldn't
  should not — shouldn't

He **would** talk to her. (Ele falaria com ela.)
Would you buy that book? (Você compraria aquele livro?)
He **should** not invite her. (Ele não deveria convidá-la.)

PRACTICE (Respostas na pág. 100)

1. Observe the song titles. Underline the modal auxiliaries.

1. <u>Wouldn't</u> It Be Nice?
2. Who Can It Be Now?
3. My Heart Will Go On
4. Love Will Keep Us Alive
5. Love Can Build A Bridge
6. I Would Do Anything For Love But I Won't Do That
7. I Will Survive
8. You Should Be Dancing
9. I Could Have Danced All Night
10. Could I Have This Dance
11. I Would Not Be Alone

12. Can't Buy Me Love
13. I Will Always Love You
14. I Can See Clearly Now
15. You Must Remember This...
16. I Can't Help Falling In Love
17. Who'll Stop The Rain
18. I Can't Take My Eyes Off Of You
19. I Can See Clearly Now The Rain Is Gone
20. You Must Have Been A Beautiful Baby

2. Check the correct meaning.

1. The puppy can sit on command.
   ☑ ability   ☐ permission

2. You could go across the swamp, but I advise against it.
   ☐ possibility   ☐ deduction

3. Garred should arrive in a few minutes.
   ☐ permission   ☐ prediction

4. Since all birds fly, this ostrich must fly.
   ☐ deduction   ☐ ability

5. You might consider painting your house white.
   ☐ condition   ☐ suggestion

6. You may meet him at the restaurant.
   ☐ ability   ☐ probability

3. Choose the correct alternative.

1. They have been walking for hours. They _____ be very tired.
   ☐ can   ☑ must

2. You _____ enter the country without a visa.
   ☐ can't   ☐ must

3. Students _____ only borrow two books at a time.
   ☐ may   ☐ might

4. He left two hours ago. He _____ have arrived by now.
   ☐ can   ☐ must

5. The doctor said I _____ lose some weight. I'm too heavy.
   ☐ can   ☐ must

6. You _____ well be right.
   ☐ may   ☐ might

7. The restaurant is always empty – it _____ be much good.
   ☐ can't   ☐ couldn't

8. That's the door bell. Who _____ it be?
   ☐ can   ☐ must

9. They're still missing, so they _____ have died.
   ☐ may   ☐ might

10. I don't believe you – you _____ be joking.
    ☐ should   ☐ must

11. You _____ have told me earlier!
    ☐ may   ☐ might

12. You _____ smoke in the cinema.
    ☐ can't   ☐ might not

13. _____ you turn it down a bit please?
    ☐ Can   ☐ May

14. The teacher says we _____ leave when we've finished.
    ☐ may   ☐ would

15. They _____ be on holiday, but I'm not sure.
    ☐ can   ☐ may

16. From the way he speaks, he _____ be from London.
    ☐ would   ☐ could

17. The weather _____ be better tomorrow.
    ☐ can   ☐ may

18. _____ you speak Japanese?
    ☐ Can   ☐ May

19. It _____ be very expensive, but it's much better than the others.
    ☐ may   ☐ might

20. _____ you smell something burning?
    ☐ Can   ☐ Must

4. Answer the questions. Use short answers.

1. Can dogs fly?   No, they _can't_____.
2. Would you like to travel by bus?   No, I _____.
3. Will they get married?   Yes, they _____.
4. Could you swim when you were young?   No, I _____.
5. Will they help me?   No, they _____.
6. May I open the window?   Yes, you _____.
7. Can he really build houses?   Yes, he _____.
8. Could they come back another day?   Yes, they _____.
9. Take another look, I may be correct.   No, you _____.
10. Would he come if we asked him to?'   Yes, he _____.

Tempos verbais

SIMPLE TENSES

O 'Simple Present', 'Simple Past' e 'Simple Future' situam ações, fatos, opiniões no tempo presente, passado ou futuro. Em inglês, nem sempre o tempo expresso é o que está aparentemente evidente. Indicações por vezes sutis podem levar o aluno de língua estrangeira a não perceber claramente o período de tempo expresso:

*The train **leaves** tomorrow morning.*
(O trem parte amanhã de manhã.)

Observe a forma:

simple present	VERBO + s/es	*I work, he work**s***
		(Eu trabalho, ele trabalha)
simple past	VERBO + d/ed	*I work**ed***
		(Eu trabalhei/trabalhava)
	VERBO irregular	*I **slept***
		(Eu dormi/dormia)
simple future	will + VERBO	*I **will** work*
		(Trabalharei/Vou trabalhar)

PROGRESSIVE TENSES

Os tempos 'progressive' ou 'continuous' mostram uma ação em andamento, por um período de tempo, em um determinado momento (presente, passado ou futuro). São formados por BE + PRESENT PARTICIPLE[1] de um verbo.

Observe a forma:

present progressive	am/is/are + VERBO + ing	*I **am** study**ing***. (Estou estudando.)
past progressive	was/were + VERBO + ing	*He **was** sleep**ing***. (Ele estava dormindo.)
future progressive	will be + VERBO + ing	*They **will be** travel**ing***. (Ela estará viajando.)

VERBOS RARAMENTE USADOS EM PROGRESSIVE TENSES'

Como tais tempos sugerem que algo acontece, ou é verdadeiro apenas por um tempo limitado, alguns verbos, por seu significado, raramente são usados nesse tipo de construção:

sentidos – see   hear   smell   notice   recognize   seem

emoção – like   dislike   desire   wish   care   love   hate   refuse   want   forgive   prefer

razão – think   feel   realize   understand   believe   expect   know   mean   suppose   mind   remember   forget   agree

posse – belong   possess   owe   own   keep

I don't believe it.
(Não estou acreditando.)

Do you understand?
(Você está entendendo?)

[1]. particípio presente = verbo + ing

PERFECT TENSES

Os tempos 'perfect' geralmente expressam as consequências de um estado ou ação anterior. São formados por HAVE + PAST PARTICIPLE[2] de um verbo.

Observe:

present perfect	have/has + VERBO no particípio passado	*I **have studied** hard.* (Estudei/Estudo/ Tenho estudado muito.)
past perfect	had + VERBO no particípio passado	*He **had slept** late* (Ele tinha dormido tarde.)
future perfect	will have + VERBO no particípio passado	*They **will have arrived**.* (Eles terão chegado.)

PERFECT PROGRESSIVE TENSES

Os tempos 'perfect progressive' expressam ações incompletas ou em andamento. De modo geral, enfatizam a forma como o sujeito passa o tempo. São formados por HAVE BEEN + PRESENT PARTICIPLE[3] de um verbo.

Observe:

present perfect progressive	have/has been + VERBO + ing	*I **have been** studying hard.* (Tenho estado estudando muito./ Tenho estudado muito.)

---

2. O particípio passado dos verbos regulares termina em d/ed; os verbos irregulares têm forma própria (ver pág. 113).
3. particípio presente = verbo + ing

past perfect progressive	had been + VERBO + ing	*He **had been** sleeping late.* (Ele tinha andado dormindo tarde.)
future perfect progressive	will have been + VERBO + ing	*They **will have been** complaining.* (Eles terão estado reclamando/ terão reclamado.)

CONDITIONAL TENSES

Os 'conditional tenses' são usados em frases condicionais (conditional sentences).

Observe:

simple	would + VERBO	*I **would** work.* (Eu trabalharia.)
progressive	would be + VERBO + ing	*I **would be** working.* (Eu estaria trabalhando.)
perfect	would have + VERBO	*I **would have** worked.* (Eu teria trabalhado.)
perfect progressive	would have been + VERBO + ing	*I **would have been** working.* (Eu teria estado trabalhando.)

Simple Present

He usually **walks** to school.
They **arrive** home at 4:00 every day.

Usamos o **Simple Present** para expressar ações usuais, costumeiras, hábitos, generalizações, acontecimentos reconhecidos como verdades, resumos de histórias, acontecimentos programados.

Nem sempre o simple present expressa o tempo presente e nem sempre a melhor tradução é a do presente simples. O contexto, advérbios e demais palavras sempre devem ser considerados.

*We **live**[1] in Brazil.* (Moramos/Estamos morando no Brasil.)
*I **understand**[1].* (Entendo/Estou entendendo.)
*We **study** near here.* (Estudamos/Estamos estudando perto daqui.)
*I hope it **rains** tomorrow.* (Espero que chova amanhã.)
*He **doesn't play** soccer on Saturdays.*
(Ele não joga/não está jogando futebol aos sábados.)
*Do you always **get** up early?* (Você sempre levanta cedo?)
*The bus **leaves** at 8:00.* (O ônibus sai às 8.)
*Babies **love** milk.* (Bebês adoram leite.)
*The sun **rises** in the east.* (O sol nasce no leste.)
*She **looks** at him and **leaves** the room.* (Ela olha para ele e sai da sala.)

Advérbios ou **expressões adverbiais** muito usados com esse tempo verbal:

often, frequently (frequentemente)   *usually* (usualmente)
never (nunca)   *generally* (geralmente)
sometimes (às vezes)   *always* (sempre)
rarely, hardly ever (raramente)   *every day, on Mondays* etc.

---

1. Ver verbos não usados com a terminação **ing** na pág. 22.

I **often** walk to school. (Vou a pé para a escola frequentemente.)
They **usually** know the answers. (Eles usualmente sabem as respostas.)
He **generally** arrives late. (Ele geralmente chega tarde.)
She **rarely** listens to me. (Ela raramente me ouve.)
Sometimes, we talk about work. (Às vezes, conversamos sobre trabalho.)
You **never** help him. (Você nunca o ajuda.)
We study Greek **every day**. (Estudamos/Estamos estudando grego todos os dias.)

AS FORMAS

a. **afirmativa** – VERBO + s/es na 3ª pessoa do singular

run
I run   *we run*
you run   *you run*
he, she, it runs   *they run*

b. **negativa** – coloca-se DO NOT² ou DOES NOT antes do verbo principal.

*We **do not** run.*   *He **does not** run³.*
(Nós não corremos.)   (Ele não corre.)

c. **interrogativa** – coloca-se DO ou DOES antes do sujeito.

***Do** you run?*   ***Does** she run?*
(Você corre?)   (Ela corre?)

d. **interrogativa-negativa** – coloca-se DON'T ou DOESN'T antes do sujeito.

***Don't** you run?*   ***Doesn't** she run?*
(Você não corre?)   (Ela não corre?)

2. **Do**, verbo auxiliar, não é traduzido.
3. Quando **do** é o auxiliar, o verbo principal fica na forma base.

e. **formas abreviadas:**

does not – doesn't   *do not – don't*

A **grafia** do verbo na 3ª pessoa do singular – he, she, it – deve ser observada:

a. a maioria dos verbos recebe **s**:
   *run**s**   work**s**   stop**s**   hit**s**   play**s***

b. verbos terminados em **ss**, **sh**, **ch**, **x**, **z**, **o** recebem **es**:
   *miss**es**   brush**es**   teach**es**   mix**es**   buzz**es**   do**es***

c. verbos terminados em *consoante* + *y* trocam o *y* por *i* e recebem **es**:
   *stud**y** – stud**ies**   tr**y** – tr**ies**   den**y** – den**ies***

A **pronúncia** dos verbos na 3ª pessoa do singular também deve ser observada:

som final	pronúncia – 3ª pessoa
|p|, |t|, |k|	|s|: *stops hits packs*
|s|, |z|, |sh|, |ch|, |j|	|**iz**|: *misses rises wishes watches judges*
demais sons finais	|**z**|: *dreams rides pays*

PRACTICE (Respostas na pág. 101)

1. Rewrite the sentences. Use the given subject.

   I love Paris.
   Cindy loves Paris   .

1. *They wish you a happy birthday.*
   Jane _____
2. *The boys cry when they see me.*
   The boy _____
3. *We always try to catch that bus.*
   Albert _____
4. *My parents teach chemistry.*
   Mom _____
5. *Alex always misses the bus.*
   My friends _____
6. *I always study hard but I have bad grades.*
   John _____
7. *My cat runs after the dog every morning.*
   My cats _____
8. *We watch the ballet when possible.*
   Karen _____
9. *They enjoy going to the park.*
   Little Tom _____
10. *She has no time to talk to you.*
    I _____

2. Choose the correct interrogative form.

1. *He studies English near his house.*
   (a) ☐ *Does he studies English near his house?*
   (b) ☑ *Does he study English near his house?*

2. *They always get late to work.*
   (a) ☐ *Do they always get late to work?*
   (b) ☐ *Don't they gets late to work?*

3. *We travel around the world once a year.*
   (a) ☐ *Do you travel around the world once a year?*
   (b) ☐ *Does you travel around the world once a year?*

4. *The baby sleeps early.*
   (a) ☐ *Does the baby sleep early?*
   (b) ☐ *Does the baby sleeps early?*

5. *Sally washes the dishes before going to sleep.*
   (a) ☐ *Do Sally washes the dishes before going to sleep?*
   (b) ☐ *Does Sally wash the dishes before going to sleep?*

3. Answer the questions. Write short answers.

1. *Do you like tea?*
   Yes, I <u>do</u>   .
2. *Do they live near here?*
   No, they <u>don't</u>   .
3. *Does she speak Japanese?*
   Yes, she _____ .
4. *Do we know you?*
   Yes, you _____ .
5. *Does the bus stop here?*
   No, it _____ .

4. Choose the adequate verb form.

1. *We always _____ early.*
   ☑ *get up*   ☐ *gets up*   ☐ *don't get up*

2. *She _____ dogs.*
   ☐ *don't like*   ☐ *doesn't like*   ☐ *doesn't likes*

3. *We _____ time to do it.*
   ☐ *don't have*   ☐ *doesn't have*   ☐ *doesn't has*

4. *My friends _____ here often.*
   ☐ *come*   ☐ *comes*   ☐ *no comes*

5. She _____ a boyfriend.
   ☐ don't has   ☐ doesn't has   ☐ doesn't have

6. I _____ my money at home.
   ☐ don't keep   ☐ don't keeps   ☐ doesn't keep

7. Often, she _____ TV in the afternoon when she is home.
   ☐ does watch   ☐ watches   ☐ watch

8. It usually _____ in December.
   ☐ don't rain   ☐ doesn't rains   ☐ doesn't rain

9. Why do they _____ their homework in the evening?
   ☐ do   ☐ don't   ☐ does

10. They _____ handball every Friday.
    ☐ plays   ☐ play   ☐ doesn't play

5. Read the sentences. Observe the pronunciation.

11. Jennifer speaks English well.   speaks /s/
12. My sister gets to school at 7:00.   _____
13. He watches TV in the evening.   _____
14. The bus stops here.   _____
15. The train leaves at 4:00.   _____
16. He eats lobster for lunch.   _____
17. He dances quite well.   _____
18. She teaches me English.   _____
19. Dad drives to work in the morning.   _____
20. Jane dreams about going to London.   _____

Simple Past

He **walked** to school yesterday.
They **left** home at 4:00 last Sunday.

Usamos o **Simple Past** para expressar hábitos ou situações passadas e ações finalizadas no passado. O contexto ou expressões adverbiais devem indicar quando a ação se realizou.

*He **studied** French on Mondays.* (Ele estudava/estudou francês às segundas.)
*We **lived** in Brazil when we were young.* (Moramos no Brasil quando jovens.)
*I **cooked** chicken for dinner.* (Assei um frango para o jantar.)

Advérbios ou **expressões adverbiais** muito usados com esse tempo verbal:

yesterday (ontem) *last...* (último...)
...ago (...atrás) *before* (antes de)

*I saw you at school **yesterday**.* (Vi você na escola ontem.)
*He didn't play soccer **last** Saturday.* (Ele não jogou futebol sábado passado.)
*The bus left two hours **ago**.* (O ônibus partiu há duas horas/duas horas atrás.)
*I closed the window **before** leaving.* (Fechei a janela antes de sair.)

AS FORMAS

Em inglês há verbos regulares e irregulares (regular and irregular verbs). Os regulares seguem regras para a formação do passado e particípio passado enquanto que os irregulares têm formas próprias.

a. **afirmativa**

   regular verb: VERBO + ***d/ed***
   irregular verb: (ver pág. 113)

work	*write*
*I work**ed***	*I **wrote***
you worked	*you wrote*
he, she, it worked	*he, she, it wrote*
we worked	*we wrote*
you worked	*you wrote*
they worked	*they wrote*

b. **negativa** – coloca-se DID NOT[1] antes do verbo principal.

   *I **did not** work*[2].   *He **did not** leave.*
   (Eu não trabalhei.)   (Ele não saiu.)

c. **interrogativa** – coloca-se DID antes do sujeito.

   ***Did** you work?*   ***Did** she leave?*
   (Você trabalhou?)   (Ela saiu?)

d. **interrogativa-negativa** – coloca-se DIDN'T antes do sujeito.

   ***Didn't** you work?*   ***Didn't** she leave?*
   (Você não trabalhou?)   (Ela não saiu?)

e. **forma abreviada:**

   did not — didn't

---

1. **Do**, verbo auxiliar, não é traduzido.
2. Quando **do** é o auxiliar, o verbo principal fica na forma base.

A **grafia** de verbos regulares no passado deve ser observada:

a. a maioria dos verbos recebe *e* ou *ed* sem sofrer outras alterações:
   work**ed**   play**ed**   danc**ed**   lov**ed**

b. verbos terminados em **consoante** + **y** recebem *ed* e trocam o *y* por *i*:
   stud**y** – stud**ied**   tr**y** – tr**ied**   den**y** – den**ied**

c. verbos terminados por sílaba tônica, formada por consoante--vogal-consoante, dobram a consoante e recebem *ed*:
   permit – permi**tt**ed   drop – dro**pp**ed   occur – occu**rr**ed

A **pronúncia** dos verbos regulares no passado também deve ser observada:

som final	pronúncia
|t|, |d|	|id|: *heated loaded*
|p|, |k|, |s|, |sh|, |ch|, | f |	|t|: *stopped packed missed wished watched laughed*
demais sons finais	|d|: *breathed blazed filled tried*

PRACTICE (Respostas na pág. 102)

1. Complete the sentences with the correct form of the regular verbs in parentheses.

    1. (watch) We _____ watched _____ TV yesterday in the afternoon.
    2. (rain) It _____ a lot last month.
    3. (play) They _____ volleyball two weeks ago.
    4. (stop) He _____ writing when I arrived.
    5. (laugh) The kids _____ when he entered the room.
    6. (dance) She _____ all night. She was very happy.

33

7. (study – live) I _____ French when I _____ in France.
8. (try) I _____ to talk to her but I didn't meet her.
9. (cook) He _____ some fish for dinner.
10. (bake) Mom _____ a cake for my birthday.

2. Complete the sentences with the correct form of the irregular verbs in parentheses.[3]

1. (have) He ____had____ a black and white dog many years ago.
2. (do – go) The kids _____ their homework and _____ to the park.
3. (get up) You _____ very late yesterday.
4. (take) She _____ the wrong bus to school.
5. (come) Sue and Paul _____ here last night.
6. (buy) I _____ some meat for dinner.
7. (put) He _____ the lettuce in the refrigerator.
8. (read) We _____ grandma's letter yesterday.
9. (break) He _____ mom's crystal cup.
10. (teach) We _____ English last year.

3. Answer the questions. Write short answers.

1. Did Meg go to the bookstore?
   Yes, _she did_____.
2. Did they build their house last year?
   Yes, _____.
3. Did you meet Joan yesterday?
   No, _____.
4. Did Helen wake up at seven?
   No, _____.
5. Did your sisters go to France?
   Yes, _____.

3. Ver verbos irregulares na pág. 113.

4. Give complete answers to the questions. Use the words in parentheses.

1. *Where did he go? (the gym)*
   He went to the gym   .
2. *What did she buy? (some eggs)*
   _____.
3. *When did you lose your bag? (yesterday)*
   _____.
4. *When did they leave? (an hour ago)*
   _____.
5. *How many pills did you take? (two)*
   _____.
6. *How much did the shirt cost? ($70)*
   _____.
7. *What time did you arrive? (at 7)*
   _____.
8. *Where did you live? (in Greece)*
   _____.
9. *What did Tom see? (a ghost)*
   _____.
10. *How did you go there? (on foot)*
    _____.

5. Choose the correct alternative to complete the sentences.

1. *Your friends _____ the room a few minutes ago.*
   ☑ *left*   ☐ *leave*   ☐ *didn't left*

2. *My TV _____ working last night.*
   ☐ *stopt*   ☐ *stopped*   ☐ *didn't stopped*

3. *Did we _____ near the beach when we were children?*
   ☐ *lived*   ☐ *live*   ☐ *left*

35

4. He didn't _____ the project last night.
   ☐ finishes   ☐ finished   ☐ finish

5. My daughter _____ her notebook in the lab last week.
   ☐ leaves   ☐ didn't lived   ☐ left

6. He _____ smoking last year.
   ☐ gave up   ☐ give up   ☐ not give up

7. Ray _____ home some minutes ago.
   ☐ not go   ☐ went   ☐ did went

8. My uncle _____ before I was born.
   ☐ die   ☐ don't die   ☐ died

9. Did you _____ to the concert last Sunday?
   ☐ went   ☐ left   ☐ go

10. They _____ me some games last night.
    ☐ teach   ☐ didn't taught   ☐ showed

11. We _____ to the seaside last summer.
    ☐ was   ☐ didn't go   ☐ not went

12. I didn't _____ the last question.
    ☐ understood   ☐ understand   ☐ not understand

13. Columbus _____ America more than 500 years ago.
    ☐ see   ☐ didn't saw   ☐ discovered

14. Your brother _____ me on the head last class.
    ☐ hat   ☐ hut   ☐ hit

15. I brought 10 sandwiches; how many did you _____ ?
    ☐ bring   ☐ brought   ☐ bought

6. Read the sentences. Observe the pronunciation.

1. They watched the match together.   watched |t|
2. The bus stopped near the mall.
3. He dances quite well.
4. Jane dreams about going to London.
5. I parked the car at the car entrance.
6. You needed me.
7. He tried to read the newspaper.
8. The boy climbed the tree.
9. The dentist pulled out two of my teeth.
10. She said she hated me.

Simple Future

He **will walk** to school tomorrow.
They **will leave** home at 4:00 next Sunday.

Usamos o **Simple Future** para descrever atividades futuras, expressar decisões tomadas sobre o futuro, forte intenção, previsões corriqueiras, fazer um pedido, oferecer ajuda. Geralmente é o contexto que evidencia o tipo de previsão ou intenção.

*We **will visit** grandma tomorrow.* (Visitaremos a vovó amanhã.)
*I **will study** harder next semester.* (Estudarei mais no próximo semestre.)
*They **will arrive** before dinner.* (Eles chegarão/chegam antes do jantar.)
***Will** you **prepare** dinner, please.* (Prepare o jantar, por favor.)
*I **will teach** you about verb tenses.* (Vou te ensinar os tempos verbais.)

Advérbios ou **expressões adverbiais** muito usados com esse tempo verbal:

tomorrow (amanhã)   *next...* (próximo...)
in... (em...)   *after...* (após...)

*I will see you at school **tomorrow**.* (Vejo você na escola amanhã.)
*He will not play soccer **next** Saturday.* (Ele não vai jogar futebol no próximo sábado.)
*The bus will leave **in** ten minutes.* (O ônibus vai partir/parte em 10 minutos.)
*I will watch the movie **after** dinner.* (Veremos o filme após o jantar.)

AS FORMAS

a. **afirmativa**: will + VERBO

I **will/shall**[1] work
you will work
he, she, it will work

we will/shall work
you will work
they will work

b. **negativa** – coloca-se WILL NOT antes do verbo principal.

I will not work.
(Não vou trabalhar.)

He will not leave.
(Ele não vai sair.)

c. **interrogativa** – coloca-se WILL antes do sujeito.

Will you work?
(Você vai trabalhar?)

Will she leave?
(Ela vai sair?)

d. **interrogativa-negativa** – coloca-se WON'T antes do sujeito.

Won't you work?
(Você não vai trabalhar?)

Won't she leave?
(Ela não vai sair?)

e. **formas abreviadas**:

will/shall — 'll   will not — won't   shall not — shan't

Nota: o futuro também pode ser expresso através de **shall** (formal), be *going to* e do **present progressive**.

Shall we **leave** now, please?
(Vamos sair agora, por favor?)
Shall I **carry** this for you?
(Posso carregar/quer que carregue isso para você?)
It is raining. They **are going to be** late.
(Está chovendo. Eles vão se atrasar.)
We **are meeting** our friends after class.
(Vamos encontrar nossos amigos após a aula.)

1. **Shall** (inglês formal) pode ser usado apenas com as primeiras pessoas: I e we

PRACTICE (Respostas na pág. 103)

1. Complete the sentences with the simple **future tense** of the verbs in parentheses.

   1. (translate) I _____*will translate*_____ the letter for you.
   2. (make) _____ you _____ dinner tonight?
   3. (make) I _____ some sandwiches. The kids are hungry.
   4. (not do) I _____ your composition for you.
   5. (help) _____ you _____ me move this sofá?
   6. (call) He _____ me when he arrives.
   7. (not tell) I _____ him about the party.
   8. (tell) _____ they _____ us their secret?
   9. (arrive) I'm sure they _____ after us.
   10. (be) Do you think this _____ easy to do?
   11. (be) The teacher _____ happy. All the students passed the test.
   12. (start) The party _____ at 9:00 pm.
   13. (get) The phone is ringing. I _____ it.
   14. (be) My brother _____ a great doctor.
   15. (be) The school _____ closed for a few days.

2. Complete the sentences with the ***going to*** form of the verbs in parentheses.

   1. (be) Dixon _____*is going to be*_____ the next President.
   2. (spend) I _____ my vacations in Rio.
   3. (meet) When _____ the director?
   4. (begin) My son _____ medical school next term.
   5. (make) Who _____ my birthday cake?
   6. (invite not) I _____ her for his surprise party.
   7. (drive) _____ you all the way to San Diego?
   8. (be) We _____ actors when we grow up.
   9. (not be) This _____ a very interesting year.
   10. (leave) When _____ you _____ the hotel?

11. *(rain)* Look at those clouds. It _____
12. *(not work)* We _____ next week.
13. *(not be)* The test _____ difficult.
14. *(not pass)* She _____ the test.
15. *(be)* I _____ a rich person.

Present Progressive

He **is walking** to school now.
They **are playing** soccer at this moment.

Usamos o **Present Progressive** para expressar ações da atualidade ou ações ocorrendo no momento da fala. Pode também expressar eventos futuros planejados.

> We **are taking** music lessons this year. (Estamos tendo aulas de música este ano.)
> I **'m studying** English now. (Estou estudando inglês agora.)
> She **is leaving** next week. (Ela parte na próxima semana.)

Advérbios ou **expressões adverbiais** muito usados com esse tempo verbal:

> *now* (agora) *at the moment* (no momento)
> *at present* (no presente)

> He is washing his car **now**. (Ele está lavando o carro agora.)
> They are talking to Jane **at the moment**.
> (Eles estão falando com Jane no momento.)

AS FORMAS

a. **afirmativa**: am/is/are + VERBO + ing

> I **am** study**ing**   we are studying
> you are studying   you are studying
> he, she, it is studying   they are studying

b. **negativa** – acrescenta-se NOT ao verbo auxiliar:

*He **is not** studying.* (Ele não está estudando.)

c. **interrogativa** – coloca-se o auxiliar antes do sujeito:

***Is** she studying?* (Ela está estudando?)

d. **interrogativa-negativa** – coloca-se o verbo auxiliar na forma negativa e abreviada antes do sujeito:

***Isn't** she studying?* (Ela não está estudando?)

e. **formas abreviadas**:

am — 'm	*is — 's*
are — 're	*am not — 'm not*
is not — isn't	*are not — aren't*

A **grafia** do VERBO + ing[1] deve ser observada:

a. a maioria dos verbos recebe *ing* sem sofrer transformações:
*work**ing**   play**ing**   study**ing**   eat**ing***

b. verbos terminados em *e* perdem o *e*:
*hav**e** – hav**ing**   tak**e** – tak**ing**   writ**e** – writ**ing***
mas, *b**e** – b**eing**   agre**e** – agre**eing**   se**e** – se**eing***

c. verbos terminados em *ie* trocam o *ie* por *y*:
*d**ie** – d**ying**   t**ie** – t**ying**   l**ie** – l**ying***

d. verbos terminados por sílaba tônica, formada por *consoante/vogal/consoante*, dobram a consoante:

---

1. Ver verbos não usados com a forma ing na pág. 22.

hit — hi**tt**ing   cut — cu**tt**ing   begin — begi**nn**ing
mas, gro**w** — gro**w**ing   mi**x** — mi**x**ing

PRACTICE (Respostas na pág. 104)

1. Rewrite the verbs adding *–ing*.

    1. *argue*   *arguing*
    2. *run*
    3. *admit*
    4. *stop*
    5. *love*
    6. *hate*
    7. *get*
    8. *begin*
    9. *study*
    10. *try*
    11. *say*
    12. *die*
    13. *fix*
    14. *snow*

2. Complete the sentences with the **present progressive** form of the verbs in parentheses.

    1. (study) This month, I _____ am studying _____ Spanish.
    2. (come) _____ you _____ to see us next month?
    3. (wait) They _____ for you now.
    4. (make) I _____ a lot of progress at the moment.
    5. (live) _____ they really _____ abroad?
    6. (watch – play) Is grandma _____ TV?
       No, she _____ cards.
    7. (run neg. – swim) He _____ in the park. He _____ in the lake.

8. (lie) I don't believe you. You _____
9. (get) Let's go home. It _____ late.
10. (write) Who _____ the message?

3. Choose the correct alternative.

1. The children _____ , they _____ .
   ☑ aren't playing – are sleeping   ☐ don't play – aren't sleeping

2. _____ it _____ now?
   ☐ Is – rain   ☐ Is – raining

3. What _____ the baby _____? He _____ your magazine.
   ☐ is – doing/is tearing up   ☐ does – doing/tears

4. I _____ a play by Shakespeare.
   ☐ is writing   ☐ am reading

5. Our students _____ two-zero.
   ☐ is not winning   ☐ are winning

6. Mom _____ the flowers, she _____ the newspaper.
   ☐ isn't watering – is reading   ☐ is not watering – isn't reading.

7. _____ the Browns _____ dinner with us tonight?
   ☐ Aren't – have   ☐ Are – having

8. We _____ English at the moment.
   ☐ are learning   ☐ aren't learn

9. Who _____ the cookery book?
   ☐ writing   ☐ is writing

10. I _____ for Berlin on the last flight.
    ☐ am leaving   ☐ don't leaving

4. Answer the questions. Use the words in parentheses.

1. *What are you doing?*
   (answer the questions) <u>*I am answering the questions*</u>   .
2. *What are the children doing?*
   (play soccer) _____.
3. *What is grandma doing?*
   (swim) _____.
4. *Is Sue leaving now?*
   (Yes) _____.
5. *Are the boys wearing jeans?*
   (No) _____.

Past Progressive

He **was walking** to school one hour ago.
They **were playing** soccer yesterday morning.

Usamos o **Past Progressive** para expressar situações que estavam em andamento ou ações que estavam em andamento quando algo aconteceu.

*The day was dark. It **was raining** hard.*
(O dia estava escuro. Estava chovendo muito.)
*I **was reading** when the bell rang.*
(Eu estava lendo quando a campainha soou.)

Advérbios ou **expressões adverbiais** muito usados com esse tempo verbal:

when (quando)   while (enquanto)   at... o'clock, yesterday etc.

*They were talking to Jane **when** I arrived.*
(Eles estavam falando com Jane quando cheguei).
*She was sleeping **while** we were watching TV.*
(Ela estava dormindo enquanto eles assistiam à TV.)
***At 4:00** he was washing his car.*
(Às 4 horas ele estava lavando o carro.)

AS FORMAS

a. **afirmativa**: was/were + VERBO + ing

*I **was** study**ing***	*we were studying*
you were studying	*you were studying*
he, she, it was studying	*they were studying*

b. **negativa** – acrescenta-se NOT ao verbo auxiliar:

*He **was not** studying.* (Ele não estava estudando.)

c. **interrogativa** – coloca-se o auxiliar antes do sujeito:

***Was** she studying?* (Ela estava estudando?)

d. **interrogativa-negativa** – coloca-se o verbo auxiliar na forma negativa e abreviada antes do sujeito:

***Weren't** you studying?* (Você não estava estudando?)

e. **formas abreviadas:**

was not — wasn't   were not — weren't

A **grafia** do VERBO + ing deve ser observada (ver pág. 86).

PRACTICE (Respostas na pág. 105)

1. Rewrite the sentences according to the words in parentheses.

1. *She was wearing her wedding ring.*
   (negative) She wasn't wearing her wedding ring   .
2. *They were running across the street.*
   (interrogative) _____ .
3. *We weren't hitting the little boy.*
   (affirmative) _____ .
4. *Was he trying to cross the river?*
   (negative) _____ .

5. *I was waiting for you.*
   (interrogative) _____ .

2. Supply the **past progressive** form of the verbs in parentheses.

1. (read) I _____was reading_____ the newspaper when he came in.
2. (not look) He took another coffee when you _____ .
3. (shine) The sun _____ when we went out.
4. (have) The light went out while we _____ dinner.
5. (get) The bus started while the old lady _____ on.
6. (live) We _____ in Germany when the war began.
7. (sleep) When Mom arrived home I _____ still _____ .
8. (sit) They _____ in the garden when the house fell down.
9. (cross) He _____ the street when he saw the accident.
10. (snow) When I got up this morning, it _____ .

3. Choose the correct alternative.

1. *When we _____ her, she was wearing her wedding ring.*
   ☐ see   ☑ saw   ☐ were wearing

2. *He was trying to cross the river when the police _____ him.*
   ☐ caught   ☐ catch   ☐ was catching

3. *While he was playing on the computer I _____ hard.*
   ☐ study   ☐ was studying   ☐ not study

4. *When the phone rang, I _____ the door.*
   ☐ was closing   ☐ were close   ☐ were closing

5. *We _____ home when it started to rain.*
   ☐ walk   ☐ not walk   ☐ were walking

Future Progressive

He **will be walking** to school in an hour.
They **will be playing** soccer tomorrow morning.

Usamos o **Future Progressive** para expressar situações ou ações que estarão em andamento em um certo momento futuro.

*I **will be waiting** for you tomorrow.*
(Estarei esperando por você amanhã.)
*The kids **will be sleeping** after lunch.*
(As crianças estarão dormindo/vão dormir após o almoço.)

Advérbios ou **expressões adverbiais** muito usados com esse tempo verbal:

tomorrow (amanhã) *by* (por volta de)
after (após) *before* (antes)
e também: *when, next, at... o'clock, on Monday etc.*

*He will be arriving home **at 11:00**.*
(Ele irá chegar em casa às 11:00)
*They will be getting married **by** this time tomorrow.*
(Amanhã a esta hora eles vão se casar.)

AS FORMAS

a. **afirmativa**: will be + VERBO + ing

I **will be** study**ing** we will be studying
you will be studying you will be studying
he, she, it will be studying they will be studying

b. **negativa** – acrescenta-se NOT ao auxiliar:

   He **will not** be studying. (Ele não estará estudando.)

c. **interrogativa** – coloca-se o auxiliar antes do sujeito:

   Will he be studying?

d. **interrogativa-negativa** – coloca-se o auxiliar na forma negativa e abreviada antes do sujeito:

   Won't he be studying?

e. **formas abreviadas**:

   will — 'll   will not — won't

   A **grafia** do VERBO + ing deve ser observada (ver pág. 86).

PRACTICE (Respostas na pág. 105)

1. Supply the **future progressive** of the verbs in parentheses.

   1. (fly) At this time next week she ___will be flying___ over the Pacific.
   2. (climb) By the time you get there we _____ the highest mountain.
   3. (finish) Before 10:00 tomorrow he _____ his test.
   4. (move) Some time this month we _____ to our new home.
   5. (study) Tomorrow before lunch they _____ math.

2. Rewrite the sentences according to the words in parentheses.

1. They will be waiting for you near the corner.
   (negative) _They won't be waiting for you near the corner_ .
2. Will the girls be arriving at the main entrance before 5:00?
   (affirmative) _____
3. He will be catching the train soon after dinner.
   (interrogative) _____
4. The President will be speaking to the reporters in some minutes.
   (interrogative) _____
5. I won't be sleeping by 11:00 pm this evening.
   (affirmative) _____

Present Perfect

He **has lived** in Portugal since May.
They **have run** in the park all morning.

Usamos o **Present Perfect** para expressar ações ou situações que ocorreram em um tempo não conhecido ou não mencionado, para expressar ações terminadas recentemente ou ações que começaram no passado e ainda têm algum efeito sobre o presente.

O **Present Perfect** é um tempo verbal sem equivalente em português, por isso, dependendo do contexto, pode ser traduzido pelo passado ou pelo presente.

As expressões de tempo usadas com o passado referem-se exclusivamente ao passado, ao passo que as expressões de tempo usadas com o **present perfect** devem, de alguma forma, incluir o momento presente.

Obs.: o present perfect não responde à pergunta *'When?'*.

Observe a diferença:

Simple past	Present perfect
*He **studied** French for two years.* (Ele estudou francês por dois anos. - não estuda mais)	*He **has studied** French for two years.* (Ele estuda francês há dois anos. - ele ainda estuda)
*He **lived** in Greece.* (Ele morou na Grécia. - não mora mais)	*He **has lived** in Greece.* (Ele tem morado/mora na Grécia. - ainda mora)

*I **saw** him last week.*
(Eu o vi na semana passada.)

*I **have seen** him every day.*
(Eu o vejo/tenho visto todos os dias.)

*They **played** soccer all morning.*
(Eles jogaram futebol a manhã toda.
- a manhã e o jogo já terminaram)

*They **have played** soccer all morning.*
(Eles estão jogando/tem jogado/jogaram futebol a manhã toda.
- a manhã e o jogo não terminaram)

***Did** you **go** to Rio last year?*
(Você foi ao Rio no ano passado?)

***Have** you ever **been** to Rio?*
(Você foi ao/já esteve no Rio alguma vez?)

Advérbios ou **expressões adverbiais** muito usados com esse tempo verbal:

since (desde)
many times (muitas vezes)
ever (alguma vez)
never (nunca)
already (já)

for (por)
recently (recentemente)
lately (ultimamente)
just (acabou de)
yet (ainda; já)

*I have worked here **since** yesterday.* (Trabalho aqui desde ontem.)
*He has worked here **for** two years.* (Ele trabalha aqui há dois anos.)
*We have gone to Japan **many times**.* (Fomos/temos ido ao Japão muitas vezes.)
*She has visited me **recently**.* (Ela me visitou recentemente.)
*I haven't seen Tom **lately**.* (Não tenho visto Tom ultimamente.)
*They have **never** left their country.* (Eles nunca saíram do país.)
*Have you **ever** been to Turkey?* (Você já foi à Turquia?)
*Ann has **just** arrived.* (Ann acaba de chegar.)
*I have **already** written the letter.* (Já escrevi a carta.)
*The kids haven't slept **yet**.* (As crianças ainda não dormiram.)
*Have they had lunch **yet**?* (Eles já almoçaram?)

AS FORMAS

a. **afirmativa**: have/has + VERBO no particípio passado[1]

study
*I **have studied***
you have studied
he, she, it has studied
we have studied
you have studied
they have studied

sleep
*I **have slept***
you have slept
he, she, it has slept
we have slept
you have slept
they have slept

b. **negativa** – acrescenta-se NOT ao verbo auxiliar:

*He **has not** slept well.* (Ele não dormiu/tem dormido/dorme bem)

c. **interrogativa** – coloca-se o auxiliar antes do sujeito:

***Has** he slept well?* (Ele tem dormido/dormiu bem?)

d. **interrogativa-negativa** – coloca-se o verbo auxiliar na forma negativa e abreviada antes do sujeito:

***Haven't** they slept well?* (Eles não têm dormido/ não dormiram bem?)

e. **formas abreviadas**:

have — 've
have not — haven't

has — 's
has not — hasn't

---

[1] O particípio passado dos verbos regulares termina em **d/ed** (ver grafia na pág. 85). Os verbos irregulares têm forma própria (ver pág. 113).

PRACTICE (Respostas na pág. 106)

1. Supply the **present perfect** of the verbs in parentheses. Then, translate each sentence.

   1. (meet) I ____have met____ a lot of people since I arrived.
      Conheci/Encontrei muitas pessoas desde que cheguei .

   2. (break) The boy ____has broken____ a window.
      O menino quebrou uma janela .

   3. (be) They _____ never _____ to Africa.
      _____ .

   4. (be) Where _____ you _____?
      _____ .

   5. (live) He _____ in the same house for over 40 years.
      _____ .

   6. (study) She _____ always _____ hard.
      _____ .

   7. (know) We _____ him for many years.
      _____ .

   8. (live) I _____ here since I was born.
      _____ .

   9. (call) Alex _____ just _____ me.
      _____ .

   10. (buy) She _____ a new apartment.
       _____ .

11. (move) He _____ just _____ .
    _____ .

12. (travel) I _____ by train many times.
    _____ .

2. Choose the correct alternative.

1. Winter _____ just _____ .
   - ☑ has – begun   ☐ did – began   ☐ does - begins

2. We _____ on vacation for the last two weeks.
   - ☐ were   ☐ have been   ☐ are

3. I _____ from him lately.
   - ☐ heard   ☐ haven't heard   ☐ hear

4. The show _____ yet.
   - ☐ didn't start   ☐ has start   ☐ hasn't started

5. We _____ out last Saturday night.
   - ☐ didn't go   ☐ goes out   ☐ haven't gone

6. He _____ since last year.
   - ☐ didn't talk   ☐ hasn't talked   ☐ is talking

7. I _____ unemployed since I left school.
   - ☐ was   ☐ wasn't   ☐ haven't been

8. It's the first time we _____ oysters.
   - ☐ have eaten   ☐ ate   ☐ don't eat

9. _____ he ever _____ to the USA?
   - ☐ Did – go   ☐ Do – go   ☐ Has – been

10. I _____ to many newspapers lately.
☐ have written ☐ wrote ☐ didn't write

11. He _____ many new magazines two hours ago.
☐ bought ☐ has bought ☐ have brought

12. I _____ how to skate in September, 2009.
☐ was learn ☐ have learned ☐ learned

13. We _____ to the beach because it was raining.
☐ don' go ☐ have gone ☐ didn't go

14. I _____ there at 4:00.
☐ have been ☐ was ☐ didn't be

15. I _____ here since 4:00.
☐ have been ☐ was ☐ didn't go

16. The weather _____ horrible last November.
☐ was ☐ has been ☐ haven't been

17. The weather _____ horrible since November.
☐ was ☐ weren't ☐ has been

18. They _____ a decent meal for the last two weeks.
☐ haven't had ☐ didn't have ☐ had

19. He _____ to me for an hour and a half.
☐ spoke ☐ has spoken ☐ didn't speak

20. You _____ me any money for twenty days.
☐ sent ☐ didn't send ☐ haven't sent

Past Perfect

He **had lived** in Cuba.
They **had bought** many books.

Usamos o **Past Perfect** para indicar que uma ação ocorreu antes de outra no passado.

*We **had finished** the exercise when he fainted.*
(Tínhamos terminado o exercício quando ele desmaiou.)
*The kids **had bought** some sandwiches before I arrived.*
(As crianças tinham comprado sanduíches antes que eu chegasse.)

Advérbios ou **expressões adverbiais** muito usados com esse tempo verbal:

when (quando) *before* (antes)
after (depois) *already* (já)

***When** we got to the airport, the plane had landed.*
(Quando chegamos ao aeroporto o avião tinha aterrissado.)
*She had played our song **before** we arrived.*
(Ela havia tocado nossa canção antes de chegarmos/antes da nossa chegada.)
*They started fighting **after** we had left.*
(Eles começaram a brigar depois que saímos/tínhamos saído/após nossa saída.)
*They had **already** told about the accident when we arrived.*
(Eles já haviam contado sobre o acidente quando chegamos.)

AS FORMAS

a. **afirmativa:** had + VERBO no particípio passado[1]

[1] O particípio passado dos verbos regulares termina em **d/ed** (ver grafia na pág. 85). Os verbos irregulares têm forma própria (ver pág. 113).

study	*sleep*
I **had studied**	I **had slept**
you had studied	you had slept
he, she, it had studied	he, she, it had slept
we had studied	we had slept
you had studied	you had slept
they had studied	they had slept

b. **negativa** – acrescenta-se NOT ao verbo auxiliar:

   I **had not** studied. (Eu não tinha estudado.)

c. **interrogativa** – coloca-se o auxiliar antes do sujeito:

   Had he slept? (Ele tinha dormido?)

d. **interrogativa-negativa** – coloca-se o verbo auxiliar na forma negativa e abreviada antes do sujeito:

   Hadn't they slept? (Eles não tinham dormido?)

e. **formas abreviadas**:

   had – 'd   had not – hadn't

PRACTICE (Respostas na pág. 107)

1. Supply the **past perfect** of the verbs in parentheses. Then translate the sentences.

   1. (work) I __had__ never __worked__ so hard before I joined the bank.
      Eu nunca tinha trabalhado tanto até fazer parte do banco .

   2. (leave) By the time we arrived, everyone _____ .
      _____ .

3. (win) She told me she _____ a championship ages before.
   _____.

4. (get) He bought the car after he _____ a new job.
   _____.

5. (be) They _____ on strike for a month before they reached an agreement.
   _____.

2. Choose the correct alternative.

1. I had waited for an hour before the bus finally _____ .
   ☑ arrived ☐ had arrived

2. We _____ it long before it became famous.
   ☐ read ☐ had read

3. They _____ their speech before I arrived.
   ☐ finished ☐ had finished

4. She told me his name after he _____ .
   ☐ left ☐ had left

5. He died after he _____ ill for a long time.
   ☐ was ☐ had been

6. I _____ nothing before he saw me.
   ☐ did ☐ had done

7. _____ of it until you mentioned it.
   ☐ didn't hear ☐ hadn't heard

8. I _____ enough time to finish the exam.
   ☐ didn't have ☐ hadn't have

9. He thanked me for what I _____ .
   ☐ did   ☐ had done

10. He was sorry that we _____ him.
    ☐ hurt   ☐ had hurt

3. Fill in the blanks with the verbs below.

   *found out – had gone – went – dressed – had begun – rested –
   sat down – had asked – remembered – had been – had finished – said*

1. As soon as he _____had gone_____ , I wanted to see him again.
2. They _____ after they had washed.
3. When we arrived, the meeting _____ already _____ .
4. After they had gone, I _____ and _____ .
5. Before I _____ very far, I _____ that I had lost my way.
6. It rained yesterday after it _____ dry for many days.
7. He soon _____ all he had learned at school.
8. He took the car after I _____ him not to do so.
9. We went home after we _____ our work.
10. She _____ that she had already seen the pyramids.

Future Perfect

He **will have moved** to London by May.
They **will have taken the** kids home before noon.

Usamos o **Future Perfect** para expressar qual ação se espera que aconteça dentro de um determinado tempo.

*We **will have moved** to Manaus by June.*
(Teremos mudado para Manaus até/por volta de junho.)
*He **will have learned** the alphabet before December.*
(Ele terá aprendido o alfabeto antes de/até dezembro.)

Advérbios ou **expressões adverbiais** muito usados com esse tempo verbal:

before (antes)　　　*by* (até)

*She will have sold all the paintings **before** the end of the year.*
(Ela terá vendido todas as pinturas antes do final do ano.)
*The plane will have landed **by** the time we get to the airport.*
(O avião terá pousado até chegarmos ao aeroporto.)

AS FORMAS

a. **afirmativa** – will have + VERBO no particípio passado[1]

Observe:

---

[1]. O particípio passado dos verbos regulares termina em **d/ed** (ver grafia na pág. 85). Os verbos irregulares têm forma própria (ver pág. 113).

study	*sleep*
I **will have studied**	I **will have slept**
you will have studied	you will have slept
he, she, it will have studied	he, she, it will have slept
we will have studied	we will have slept
you will have studied	you will have slept
they will have studied	they will have slept

b. **negativa** – acrescenta-se NOT ao auxiliar:

   I **will not have** studied. (Não terei estudado.)

c. **interrogativa** – coloca-se o auxiliar antes do sujeito:

   Will she have slept? (Ela terá dormido?)

d. **interrogativa-negativa** – coloca-se o verbo auxiliar na forma negativa e abreviada antes do sujeito:

   Won't they have slept? (Eles não terão dormido?)

e. **formas abreviadas**:
   will — 'll   will not — won't

PRACTICE (Respostas na pág. 107)

1. Turn into Portuguese.

1. By next January, I will have received my certificate.
   <u>Até janeiro próximo terei recebido meu diploma</u>.

2. By next December, they will have finished their English courses.
   _____.

3. By the time we go back to our country, we will have visited over 20 countries.
   _____.
4. He won't have learned Japanese before moving to Japan.
   _____.
5. I will have prepared a delicious dinner before the guests arrive.
   _____.
6. Tomorrow, by this time, she will have arrived home.
   _____.

2. Complete the sentences with the **future perfect** of the verbs in parentheses.

1. (write) By the end of the year, he _will have written_ his next novel.
2. (not forget) I hope you _____ all this by tomorrow.
3. (leave) Before you go to see them, they _____ the country.
4. (take) I _____ my examination by my birthday.
5. (eat) They _____ everything if we don't get there before eight.
6. (teach) By the end of the semester, he _____ us how to draw.
7. (be) In 2015 he _____ away for ten years.
8. (stop) I hope it _____ raining before my wedding party.
9. (sell) By next month, she _____ all her furniture.
10. (buy) When you come back we _____ the house.

3. Complete the sentences. Use the words in parentheses.

1. (meet/your boyfriend)
   By this time next week you _will have met your boyfriend_ .

2. (Our daughter/stay)
   _____ in London for five months by next Sunday.

3. (fly/more than a million miles)
   By the end of the year he _____.

4. (My niece/grow up)
   _____ by the time I return to Paris.

5. (I'm sure you/leave)
   _____ before I come back.

6. (sleep/for twenty-four hours)
   By lunch time, he _____.

7. (In January he/be)
   _____ in jail for ten years.

8. (not speak to/the pop star)
   Before you come back, we _____.

9. (The band/sing)
   _____ my favorite song before we get there.

10. (they/go/to India)
    By the time we arrive, _____.

Present/Past/ Future Perfect Progressive

He **has been living** in London since May.
They **had been playing soccer** before you arrived.
He **will have been jogging** for over an hour by 7:00.

Usamos os perfect progressive tenses geralmente para enfatizar a forma como se passa o tempo. Os 'perfect progressive tenses' são muito semelhantes em significado aos 'perfect tenses'.

Observe:

I have studied a lot. (Tenho estudado muito.)
*I **have been studying** a lot.* (Ando estudando/tenho andado estudando muito.)

He had drunk a lot. (Ele tinha bebido demais.)
*He **had been drinking** a lot.* (Ele andava bebendo demais.)

We will have learned a lot. (Teremos aprendido muito.)
*We **will have been learning** a lot.* (Teremos estado aprendendo muito.)

Advérbios ou **expressões adverbiais** usados com esses tempos verbais são os mesmos que os usados com os 'perfect tenses (ver págs 57, 63 e 67).

AS FORMAS

a. **afirmativa** – have/has been
   had been   + VERBO + ing[1]
   will have been

Present Perfect Progressive	Past Perfect Progressive	Future Perfect Progressive
I/you/we/you/they	I/you/he/she/it/ we/you/they...	I/you/he/she/it/ we/you/they...
have been working	**had been** working	**will have been** working

he, she, it
has been working

b. **negativa** – acrescenta-se NOT ao auxiliar:

   I **have not** been studying. (Não tenho estado estudando/Não tenho estudado.)

c. **interrogativa** – coloca-se o auxiliar antes do sujeito:

   Had he **been** sleeping? (Ele tinha estado dormindo?)

d. **interrogativa-negativa** – coloca-se o verbo auxiliar na forma negativa e abreviada antes do sujeito:

   Won't we have been working? (Não estaremos trabalhando?)

e. **formas abreviadas**

   have — 've   has — 's
   have not — haven't   has not — hasn't

---

1. Aqui a forma ing é a do particípio presente (ver explicação na pág. 9 e grafia na pág. 86).

had — 'd 　　　　　had not — hadn't
will — 'll 　　　　　will not — won't

PRACTICE (Respostas na pág. 108)

1. Choose the correct alternative.

1. By ten o'clock, Linda _____ for over three hours.
   ☑ will have been jogging　　☐ had being jogging

2. Next month, Glenn _____ English in the USA for two years.
   ☐ will have been studying　　☐ has been studying

3. She _____ in that house for eleven years.
   ☐ had been buying　　☐ has been living

4. By 2047, people _____ TV for 100 years.
   ☐ have been selliing　　☐ will have been watching

5. He _____ in London for five years before he decided to go back to Australia.
   ☐ had been working　　☐ has been dancing

6. He _____ driving lessons because he intended to learn how to drive.
   ☐ had been taking　　☐ will have been teaching

7. You _____ that book for weeks now.
   ☐ have been reading　　☐ had been cleaning

8. We _____ for a job since last year.
   ☐ have been looking　　☐ will have been working

9. *This place stinks! Someone _____ in here!*
   ☐ had been jogging   ☐ has been smoking

10. *They _____ to do the exercise before you helped them.*
    ☐ will have been doing   ☐ had been trying

2. Rewrite the sentences. Use the correct **perfect progressive** form of the verbs in parentheses.

1. *I (try) to finish the letter all morning.*
   I have been trying to finish the letter all morning_____ .

2. *They (ask) questions about her before the crime happened.*
   _____ .

3. *We (eat) pasta for two weeks tomorrow.*
   _____ .

4. *He (watch) that picture for hours before talking to us.*
   _____ .

5. *She (wait) for the doctor for the last two hours.*
   _____ .

Conditional Tenses

He **would move** to London if...
They **would have sold** the house if...

Geralmente usados em frases condicionais (conditional sentences), os tempos condicionais (conditional tenses) são quatro: um 'simple', um 'perfect' e dois 'progressive'.

Observe:

*I **would study** a lot if...*
(Eu estudaria muito se...)
*I **would have** studied a lot if...*
(Eu teria estudado muito se...)
*I **would be** studying a lot if...*
(Eu estaria estudando muito se...)
*I **would have been** studying a lot if...*
(Eu teria andado estudando muito se...)

AS FORMAS

a. afirmativa

Conditional Simple	*would* + verbo	I/you/he/ she/it/we/ you/they	**would go.**
Conditional Perfect	*would have* + particípio passado do verbo	I/you/he/ she/it/we/ you/they	**would have gone.**
Conditional Progressive	*would be* + verbo + *ing*	I/you/he/ she/it/we/ you/they	**would be going.**
Conditional Perfect Progressive	*would have been* + verbo + *ing*	I/you/he/ she/it/we/ you/they	**would have been going.**

b. negativa, interrogativa, interrogativa-negativa e forma abreviada – são feitas com o uso do verbo auxiliar (ver pág. 17):

*She **would not** study if...* (Ela não estudaria se...)
***Would** you have studied if...?* (Você teria estudado se...?)
***Wouldn't** you be studying if...* (Você não estaria estudando se...?)
*He **wouldn't** have been studying if...* (Ele não teria estado estudando se...)

Frases condicionais *(conditional sentences)* expressam situações hipotéticas, cuja realização é incerta. Uma frase condicional é formada por duas orações: uma oração condicional *(conditional clause)* e uma oração principal *(main clause)*

main clause	conditional clause	
I **would study**.	*If I had time.*	(Eu estudaria se tivesse tempo)

---

1. Aqui a forma 'ing' é a do present participle (ver págs 9 e 85).

76

Basicamente, há três tipos de estrutura para frases condicionais:

condição	oração principal	oração condicional
possível:	will + verbo I **will go** to the party (Irei à festa	*if he invites me.* se ele me convidar.)
improvável:	would + verbo I **would go** to the party (Eu iria à festa	*if he invited me.* se ele me convidasse.)
impossível:	would have + particípio passado I **would have gone** (Eu teria ido á festa	*if he had invited me to the party.* se ele tivesse me convidado.)

Notas:

a. Nas orações condicionais o verbo **to be** apresenta-se geralmente sob a forma **were** para todas as pessoas:

*If I **were** you, I would go.* (Se eu fosse você, eu iria)

b. A oração condicional é introduzida por 'if' (se), 'when' (quando) ou 'unless' (a não ser que):

*I will travel **when** I get rich.*
(Eu viajarei quando ficar rico)
*I won't leave **unless** he asks me to go out.*
(Vou embora a menos que ele me peça para ficar.)

PRACTICE (Respostas na pág. 109)

1. Classify the conditions:

   1. *I will fly to Peru if I have money.*
      ☑ *possible* ☐ *improbable* ☐ *impossible*

   2. *We would phone you if we had your number.*
      ☐ *possible* ☐ *improbable* ☐ *impossible*

   3. *If I were home, I'd be in bed.*
      ☐ *possible* ☐ *improbable* ☐ *impossible*

   4. *I would take it if I had the chance.*
      ☐ *possible* ☐ *improbable* ☐ *impossible*

   5. *I could have tried harder if I had wanted to.*
      ☐ *possible* ☐ *improbable* ☐ *impossible*

   6. *If I were you, I would sell it.*
      ☐ *possible* ☐ *improbable* ☐ *impossible*

   7. *I will talk to him if he comes.*
      ☐ *possible* ☐ *improbable* ☐ *impossible*

   8. *If I have time, I will help you.*
      ☐ *possible* ☐ *improbable* ☐ *impossible*

   9. *If they work hard, they may pass the examination.*
      ☐ *possible* ☐ *improbable* ☐ *impossible*

   10. *If he'd studied a little, he might have got a better grade.*
       ☐ *possible* ☐ *improbable* ☐ *impossible*

   11. *She would have been upset if it had rained.*
       ☐ *possible* ☐ *improbable* ☐ *impossible*

12. *If you'd arrived on time, you would have met her.*
    ☐ possible   ☐ improbable   ☐ impossible

13. *If you need to speak to me, call me on my mobile.*
    ☐ possible   ☐ improbable   ☐ impossible

14. *I feel sick when someone smokes near me.*
    ☐ possible   ☐ improbable   ☐ impossible

15. *I would have helped you if I had been here.*
    ☐ possible   ☐ improbable   ☐ impossible

2. Choose the correct alternative.

1. *1. If you did it, you _____ fine.*
   ☐ will feel   ☑ would feel   ☐ would have felt

2. *If I had seen her, I _____ her to ring.*
   ☐ will ask   ☐ would ask   ☐ would have asked

3. *He _____ there if he could.*
   ☐ will go   ☐ would go   ☐ would have gone

4. *If I were you I _____ in touch with a lawyer.*
   ☐ will get   ☐ would get   ☐ would have gotten

5. *If I win the lottery, I _____ on a Cruise.*
   ☐ will go   ☐ would go   ☐ would have gone

6. *We _____ him about the video if we had seen him.*
   ☐ will tell   ☐ would tell   ☐ would have told

7. *They _____ soccer tomorrow if the weather is good.*
   ☐ will play   ☐ would played   ☐ would have played

8. If they win, they _____ the World Cup.
   ☐ will get   ☐ would get   ☐ would have gotten

9. If I told you a secret, _____ you _____ it to yourself?
   ☐ will – keep   ☐ would – keep   ☐ would – have kept

10. If I were in your shoes, I _____ home.
    ☐ will go   ☐ would go   ☐ would have gone

11. He _____ the accident if he hadn't been there.
    ☐ won't see   ☐ wouldn't see   ☐ wouldn't have seen

12. You _____ well if you work harder.
    ☐ will do   ☐ would do   ☐ would have done

13. I _____ to you unless you had given me the money.
    ☐ won't talk   ☐ wouldn't talk   ☐ wouldn't have talked

14. He _____ that house unless he saves much money.
    ☐ won't buy   ☐ wouldn't buy   ☐ wouldn't have bought

15. We _____ the book if you finish writing it.
    ☐ will publish   ☐ would publish   ☐ would have published

3. Complete the sentences with the correct verb tenses.

1. (be) If he were here, things _____would be_____ different.
2. (speak) If I had had the chance, I _____ to her.
3. (get) Unless you get up earlier, you _____ to school on time.
4. (tell) If I see him, I _____ him to talk to you.
5. (do) What _____ you _____ if he arrived right now?
6. (understand) They _____ everything if you had explained it to them.
7. (not catch) You _____ the 10 o'clock bus unless you go now.

8. *(help)* I _____ *if I had been there.*
9. *(go) If you send me an invitation,* I _____ *to the party.*
10. *(sleep) The kids* _____ *late if they could.*

Apêndice: Formas Verbais Abreviadas

verbo	afirmativa	negativa
be	am: 'm is: 's are: 're	am not: 'm not is not: isn't are not: aren't was not: wasn't were not: weren't
do	—	do not: don't does not: doesn't did not: didn't
have	have: 've has: 's had: 'd	have not: haven't has not: hasn't had not: hadn't
will / shall	will: 'll shall: 'll	will not: won't shall not: shan't
would / should	would: 'd —	would not: wouldn't should not: shouldn't
can / could	— —	can not/cannot: can't could not: couldn't
may	—	—
must	—	must not: mustn't

Grafia

* **final** *s/es*

    A **grafia** do verbo na 3ª pessoa do singular – *he, she, it* – deve ser observada:

    a. a maioria dos verbos recebe **s**:
    *run**s**   work**s**   stop**s**   hit**s**   play**s***

    b. verbos terminados em **ss**, **sh**, **ch**, **x**, **z**, **o** recebem **es**:
    *mi**sses**   bru**shes**   tea**ches**   mi**xes**   bu**zzes**   d**oes***

    c. verbos terminados em **consoante** + **y** trocam o **y** por **i** e recebem **es**:
    *stud**y** – stud**ies**   tr**y** – tr**ies**   den**y** – den**ies***

* **final** *d/ed*

    A **grafia** de verbos regulares no passado deve ser observada:

    a. a maioria dos verbos recebe **e** ou **ed** sem sofrer outras alterações:
    *work**ed**   play**ed**   danc**e**d   lov**ed***

    b. verbos terminados em **consoante** + **y** recebem **ed** e trocam o **y** por **i**:
    *stud**y** – stud**ied**   tr**y** – tr**ied**   den**y** – den**ied***

    c. verbos terminados por sílaba tônica, formada por consoante-vogal-consoante, dobram a consoante e recebem **ed**:
    *permit – permi**tt**ed   drop – dro**pp**ed   occur – occu**rr**ed*

✱ final *ing*

A **grafia** do VERBO + ing deve ser observada:

a. a maioria dos verbos recebe ***ing*** sem sofrer transformações:
working   playing   studying   eating

b. verbos terminados em ***e*** perdem o ***e***:
have — hav**ing**   take — tak**ing**   write — writ**ing**
mas, be — be**ing**   agree — agree**ing**   see — see**ing**

c. verbos terminados em ie trocam o ***ie*** por ***y***:
die — d**ying**   tie — t**ying**   lie — l**ying**

d. verbos terminados por sílaba tônica, formada por consoante/vogal/consoante, dobram a consoante:
hit — hi**tt**ing   cut — cu**tt**ing   begin — begi**nn**ing
mas, grow — grow**ing**   mix — mix**ing**

Tempos Verbais Voz Passiva

A voz passiva (*passive voice*) em inglês é construída como em português.

*Ele **comeu** as maçãs. — As maçãs **foram** comidas (por ele).*

O verbo da oração fica no particípio passado enquanto o verbo ser/estar assume seu tempo. Observe as transformações dos tempos verbais.

Active Voice	Passive Voice
He _____ apples.	Apples _____ (by him).
eats (come)	are eaten (são comidas)
ate (comeu)	were eaten (foram comidas)
will eat (comerá)	will be eaten (serão comidas)
would eat (comeria)	would be eaten (seriam comidas)
He _____ apples.	Apples _____ (by him).
is eating (está comendo)	are being eaten (estão sendo comidas)
was eating (estava comendo)	were being eaten (estavam sendo comidas)
will be eating (estará comendo)	will be being eaten (estarão sendo comidas)
would be eating (estaria comendo)	would be being eaten (estariam sendo comidas)

He _____ apples.	Apples _____ (by him).
has eaten (tem comido)	have been eaten (têm sido comidas)
had eaten (tinha comido)	had been eaten (tinham sido comidas)
will have eaten (terá comido)	will have been eaten (terão sido comidas)
would have eaten (teria comido)	would have been eaten (teriam sido comidas)

He _____ apples.	Apples _____ (by him).
has been eating (tem estado comendo)	have been being eaten (têm estado sendo comidas)
had been eating (tinha estado comendo)	had been being eaten (tinham estado sendo comidas)
will have been eating (terá estado comendo)	will have been being eaten (terão estado sendo comidas)
would have been eating (teria estado comendo)	would have been being eaten (teriam estado sendo comidas)

Modo

Modo *(mood)* é uma forma verbal que mostra a maneira pela qual um pensamento é expresso. Em Inglês, como em Português, há quatro modos: indicativo, imperativo, subjuntivo e infinitivo.

* **modo indicativo** *(indicative mood)* – a maior parte das coisas que lemos, dizemos ou escrevemos está no modo indicativo. Expressa uma afirmação, negação ou questão:

    Linda is from Rio. (Linda é do Rio.)
    Birds cannot swim. (Pássaros não podem nadar.)
    Did they arrive? (Eles chegaram?)

* **modo imperativo** *(imperative mood)* – também é muito comum. Expressa comando, proibição, conselho. A afirmativa é feita pela forma base do verbo. A negatica é feita por don't + verbo:

    ***Come** back soon.* (Volte logo.)
    ***Be** careful!* (Tenha cuidado!)
    ***Don't go** away.* (Não vá embora.)

* **modo infinitivo** *(infinitive mood)* – não é usado como verbo e sim como substantivo, adjetivo ou advérbio. Pode vir com ou sem a partícula **'to'**:

    substantivo:
    ***To err** is human, **to forgive**, divine.* (Errar é humano, perdoar, divino.)

    adjetivo:
    *She is a person **to be** loved.* (Ela é alguém para ser amada.)

advérbio:
*We came **to see** you.* (Viemos ver você.)

* **modo subjuntivo** *(subjunctive mood)* – pouco empregado na fala ou na escrita do cotidiano. É usado em orações independentes ou em orações subordinadas para expressar desejo, emoção, dúvida, opinião, necessidade ou algo contrário ao fato.

    *If I **were** you, I wouldn't leave now.*
    (Se eu fosse você, não sairia agora.)
    *I wish that this car **were** cheaper.*
    (Gostaria que este carro fosse mais barato.)
    *I suggest that Garry **move** the bench to a safer place.*
    (Sugiro que Gary mova o banco para um local mais seguro.)

Prática Adicional

SIMPLE TENSES (Respostas na pág. 110)

1. Choose the correct alternative.

1. *She's Italian, she _____ from Pisa.*
   ☑ *comes* ☐ *was* ☐ *don't come*

2. *She never _____ sugar in her coffee.*
   ☐ *doesn't take* ☐ *talks* ☐ *takes*

3. *Water _____ at one hundred degrees Celsius.*
   ☐ *boiled* ☐ *boils* ☐ *boil*

4. *Smoking _____ cancer.*
   ☐ *didn't cause* ☐ *causes* ☐ *caused*

5. *He _____ silly questions last class.*
   ☐ *asked* ☐ *asks* ☐ *will ask*

6. *She _____ for her father from 2000 to 2010.*
   ☐ *worked* ☐ *work* ☐ *not will work*

7. *_____ you _____ many CDs for the party next week?*
   ☐ *did – bought* ☐ *do – buy* ☐ *did – buy*

8. *I _____ tea with sugar.*
   ☐ *don't like* ☐ *will like* ☐ *likes*

9. *We _____ home tomorrow after the graduation party.*
   ☐ *went* ☐ *will go* ☐ *go*

91

10. What _____ you _____ next Sunday?
    ☐ are – going to do   ☐ did – do   ☐ do – do

2. Supply the correct verb tense of the verbs in parentheses.

1. (put) He never _____ puts _____ salt on his food.
2. (see) I _____ tomorrow.
3. (do) What _____ you _____ this time next month?
4. (ring) He _____ me some time this afternoon.
5. (lose) She _____ her watch when she went for a walk.
6. (talk) What will you do when she arrives? I _____ to her.
7. (miss) She is always late. She _____ the bus every morning.
8. (read) We _____ that book years ago.
9. (do) The kids _____ their homework yesterday.
10. (eat) He _____ all the cream cakes last night.

3. Rewrite the sentences. Use the words in parentheses.

1. She baked a cake **yesterday**.
   (everyday) She bakes a cake everyday_____ .
2. The sun **always** shines in Egypt.
   (yesterday) _____
3. I wake up at 7:00 and have breakfast at 7:30 **every morning**.
   (tomorrow) _____
4. We **slept** there because we **were** tired.
   (neg. – neg.) _____
5. **They** don't open the door because **they** don't know you.
   (she) _____

PROGRESSIVE TENSES (Respostas na pág. 110)

1. Choose the correct alternative.

1. Look, it ____! Let's get an umbrella.
   - ☑ is raining
   - ☐ was raining
   - ☐ won't be raining

2. What ____ now? Can you see what ____?
   - ☐ is happening / is going on
   - ☐ was happening / didn't happen
   - ☐ will be happening / will be going on

3. Hurry up. The director ____ breakfast in five minutes.
   - ☐ are having
   - ☐ weren't having
   - ☐ will be having

4. He ____ your car when I saw him this morning.
   - ☐ isn't driving
   - ☐ was driving
   - ☐ will be driving

5. Gary ____ for you at the reception. He says it's important.
   - ☐ is waiting
   - ☐ was waiting
   - ☐ not will be waiting

6. Your friends ____ Mozart when I left the room.
   - ☐ aren't playing
   - ☐ were playing
   - ☐ won't be playing

7. I want to see you today. ____ by 5:00 pm?
   - ☐ Am I work
   - ☐ Were you working
   - ☐ Will you be working

8. We ____ for you when the bus arrives tonight.
   - ☐ isn't waiting
   - ☐ weren't waiting
   - ☐ will be waiting

9. I ____ at the baby when he smiled.
   - ☐ am looking
   - ☐ was looking
   - ☐ won' be looking

10. We first met while we ____ the avenue.
    - ☐ are crossing
    - ☐ were crossing
    - ☐ will be crossing

2. Supply the correct **progressive tense** – present, past or future.

1. (prepare) Yesterday at 11:00 we _____were preparing_____ lunch.
2. (wait) He _____ for her when her plane arrives.
3. (do) What _____ you _____ yesterday at 2:00?
4. (sit) She _____ in the park when the plane landed.
5. (watch) I _____ TV when she arrives tonight.
6. (discuss) Tonight they _____ their plans for the future.
7. (sleep) Be quiet. Sue _____ !
8. (say/talk) I can't hear what you _____ because everybody _____ loudly.
9. (play) The kids _____ in the garden when it began to rain.
10. (drive) At midnight tonight we _____ along the coast.
11. (fly) The birds _____. Can't you see them?
12. (study) They _____ at the library tonight, so they will not see Ann when she arrives.
13. (practice) I _____ the guitar when he came home.
14. (try) I _____ but the children are screaming downstairs.
15. (not listen) I want to tell them the true but they _____ _____ .
16. (come) While I _____ to work this morning the shops weren't open.
17. (do) You _____ a good job while we were studying at university.
18. (have) We _____ dinner when the kids started fighting.
19. (listen) _____ you _____ to the radio? What are they saying?
20. (write) I have to talk to Tom. _____ he _____ ?

PERFECT TENSES (Respostas na pág. 111)

1. Choose the correct alternative.

1. She _____ ill since Friday.
   ☑ has been   ☐ haven't been   ☐ will have been

2. He _____ breakfast before he left home this morning.
   ☐ has had   ☐ will have   ☐ had had

3. We _____ everything we need by the time you meet us.
   ☐ will have bought   ☐ had bought   ☐ have bought

4. We _____ about her for the last fifty minutes.
   ☐ will have talked   ☐ have talked   ☐ had had

5. I _____ him a new recipe before you start cooking dinner.
   ☐ had teach   ☐ have taught   ☐ will have taught

6. I _____ about him before you talked about it.
   ☐ had heard   ☐ will have hear   ☐ have heard

7. _____ you _____ the car to the mechanic yet?
   ☐ Had – take   ☐ Will – have took   ☐ Haven't – taken

8. They _____ us before you asked them to.
   ☐ hadn't helped   ☐ will have helped   ☐ have not help

9. What _____ you _____ lately?
   ☐ have – read   ☐ had – done   ☐ will – done

10. I _____ never _____ in a river.
    ☐ had – swim   ☐ have – swum   ☐ won't – swim

11. _____ you _____ to her before we met?
    ☐ Had – talked   ☐ Has – talk   ☐ Will – talk

12. We _____ as far as the lake by the time he joins us.
    ☐ will have walked   ☐ have walked   ☐ had walked

13. Next November they _____ together for fifty years.
    ☐ will have been   ☐ had been   ☐ have been

14. The children _____ the CD player before I arrived home.
    ☐ has broken   ☐ had broken   ☐ have brought

15. I _____ them since last year.
    ☐ won't have seen   ☐ had seen   ☐ haven't seen

PERFECT PROGRESSIVE TENSES (Respostas na pág. 111)

1. Supply **have/has been, had been** or **will have been**.

1. When Alex arrived I ____had been____ waiting for almost 15 minutes.
2. They _____ painting houses all summer.
3. I'm tired because I _____ running.
4. She _____ studying for 6 years before she became a doctor.
5. I _____ sleeping for 2 hours when the door bell rang.
6. By 2015 I _____ studying English for 5 years.
7. We _____ helping her for 2 years.
8. Jessica _____ working hard lately.
9. We _____ studying English for 2 years.
10. The garden is wet because it _____ raining.
11. I think the boys _____ smoking.
12. By the time they arrive, we _____ sailing for 4 hours!
13. He _____ working for the same company until he finally quit.
14. I _____ living there for years before I got married.
15. I _____ working hard for years before I got that promotion.

CONDITIONAL TENSES (Respostas na pág. 112)

1. Rewrite the sentences. Use the correct form of the verbs in parentheses.

1. (I/finish/the letter)
   <u>I will finish the letter</u> if I have time.

2. (they/go/to the movies)
   If they had money _____.

3. (I/come/sooner)
   If I had known _____.

4. (she/talk/to you)
   If she had seen you _____.

5. (We/move/to Alagoas)
   _____ if we get married.

6. (She/apologize)
   _____ if she makes a mistake.

7. (I/sell/you the house)
   _____ if I had known you wanted it.

8. (We/not work/tomorrow)
   _____ because it is a holiday.

9. (He/go away)
   If you didn't ask him to stay _____.

10. (I/not be/sad)
    _____ if I won the lottery.

Respostas dos Exercícios

INTRODUÇÃO

AUXILIARIES BE, DO, HAVE

1. (pág. 14)
1. Is
2. Is
3. Is
4. has
5. Are
6. Are
7. have
8. is
9. have
10. has

2. (pág. 14)
1. I do
2. I have
3. I am not
4. it is
5. I am
6. I am not
7. they haven't
8. they were
9. she doesn't
10. he wasn't
11. I did
12. I was
13. they aren't
14. I didn't
15. she does

3. (pág. 15)
1. was, didn't
2. Did
3. Did
4. Were
5. Was
6. Do
7. Does
8. Have
9. Has
10. Are
11. Is
12. isn't

13. had
14. Does

15. Do

MODAL AUXILIARIES

1. (pág. 17)
1. Wouldn't
2. Can
3. Will
4. Will
5. Can
6. Would/Won't
7. Will
8. Should
9. Could
10. Could
11. Would
12. Can't
13. Will
14. Can
15. Must
16. Can't
17. 'll
18. Can't
19. Can
20. Must

2. (pág. 18)
1. ability
2. possibility
3. prediction
4. deduction
5. suggestion
6. probability

3. (pág. 18)
1. must
2. can't
3. may
4. must
5. must
6. may
7. can't
8. can
9. may
10. must
11. might
12. can't
13. Can
14. may
15. may
16. could
17. may
18. Can
19. may
20. Can

4. (pág. 20)
1. can't
2. wouldn't
3. will
4. couldn't
5. won't
6. may
7. can
8. could
9. may not
10. would

SIMPLE PRESENT

1. (pág. 27)
1. wishes you a happy birthday.
2. cries when he sees me.
3. always tries to catch that bus.
4. teaches chemistry.
5. always miss the bus.
6. always studies hard but he has bad grades.
7. run after the dog every morning.
8. watches the ballet when possible.
9. enjoys going to the park.
10. I have no time to talk to you.

2. (pág. 28)
1. b
2. a
3. a
4. a
5. b

3. (pág. 29)
1. do
2. don't
3. does
4. do
5. doesn't

4. (pág. 29)
1. get up
2. doesn't like
3. don't have
4. come
5. doesn't have
6. don't keep

7. watches
8. doesn't rain
9. do
10. play

5. (pág. 30)
1. speaks /s/
2. gets /s/
3. watches /iz/
4. stops /s/
5. leaves /z/
6. eats /s/
7. dances /iz/
8. teaches /iz/
9. drives /z/
10. dreams /z/

SIMPLE PAST

1. (pág. 33)
1. watched
2. rained
3. played
4. stopped
5. laughed
6. danced
7. studied/lived
8. tried
9. cooked
10. baked

2. (pág. 34)
1. had
2. did – went
3. got up
4. took
5. came
6. bought
7. put
8. read
9. broke
10. taught

3. (pág. 34)
1. she did
2. they did
3. I didn't
4. she didn't
5. they did

4. (pág. 35)
1. He went to the gym.
2. She bought some eggs.
3. I lost my bag yesterday.
4. They left an hour ago.

5. *I took two.*
6. *It cost $70.*
7. *I arrived at 7.*
8. *I lived in Greece.*
9. *He saw a ghost.*
10. *We/I went there on foot.*

5. (pág. 35)
1. *left*
2. *stopped*
3. *live*
4. *finish*
5. *left*
6. *gave up*
7. *went*
8. *died*
9. *go*
10. *showed*
11. *didn't go*
12. *understand*
13. *discovered*
14. *hit*
15. *bring*

6. (pág. 37)
1. *watched /t/*
2. *stopped /t/*
3. *danced /t/*
4. *dreamed /d/ ou dream /t/*
5. *parked /t/*
6. *needed /id/*
7. *tried /d/*
8. *climbed /d/*
9. *pulled /d/*
10. *said /d/, hated /id/*

SIMPLE FUTURE

1. (pág. 41)
1. *will translate*
2. *Will – make*
3. *will make*
4. *won't do*
5. *Will – help*
6. *will call*
7. *won't tell*
8. *Will – tell*
9. *will arrive*
10. *will be*
11. *will be*
12. *will start*
13. *will get*
14. *will be*
15. *will be*

2. (pág. 41)
1. is going to be
2. am going to spend
3. are you going to meet
4. is going to begin
5. is going to make
6. am not going to invite
7. Are – going to drive
8. are going to be
9. is not going to be
10. are – going to leave
11. is going to rain
12. are not going to work
13. is not going to be
14. is not going to pass
15. am going to be

PRESENT PROGRESSIVE

1. (pág. 45)
1. arguing
2. running
3. admitting
4. stopping
5. loving
6. hating
7. getting
8. beginning
9. studying
10. trying
11. saying
12. dying
13. fixing
14. snowing

2. (pág. 45)
1. am studying
2. Are – coming
3. are waiting
4. am making
5. Are – living
6. watching – is playing
7. is not running – is swimming
8. are lying
9. is getting
10. is writing

3. (pág. 46)
1. aren't playing/are sleeping
2. Is – raining
3. is – doing/is tearing up
4. am reading
5. are winning
6. isn't watering/is reading
7. Are – having
8. are learning
9. is writing
10. am leaving

4. (pág. 47)
1. I am answering the questions.
2. They are playing soccer.
3. She is swimming.
4. Yes, she is.
5. No, they aren't.

PAST PROGRESSIVE

1. (pág. 50)
1. She wasn't wearing her wedding ring.
2. Were they running across the street?
3. We were hitting the little boy.
4. He wasn't trying to cross the river.
5. Were you waiting for me?

2. (pág. 51)
1. was reading
2. were not looking
3. was shining
4. were having
5. was getting
6. were living
7. was – sleeping
8. were sitting
9. was crossing
10. was snowing

3. (pág. 51)
1. saw
2. caught
3. was studying
4. was closing
5. were walking

FUTURE PROGRESSIVE

1. (pág. 54)
1. will be flying
2. will be climbing
3. will be finishing
4. will be moving
5. will be studying

2. (pág. 55)
1. They won't be waiting for you near the corner.
2. The girls will be arriving at the main entrance before 5:00.
3. Will he be catching the train soon after dinner?
4. Will the President be speaking to the reporters in some minutes?
5. I will be sleeping by 11:00 pm this evening.

PRESENT PERFECT

1. (pág. 60)
1. have met (Conheci/Encontrei muitas pessoas desde que cheguei)
2. has broken (O menino quebrou uma janela)
3. have – been (Eles nunca estiveram na África)
4. have – been (Por onde você andava/tem andado)
5. has lived (Ele mora na mesma casa há mais de 40 anos)
6. has – studied (Ela sempre estudou muito)
7. have known (Nós o conhecemos há muitos anos)
8. have lived (Moro aqui desde que nasci)
9. has – called (Alex acaba/acabou de telefonar)
10. has bought (Ela comprou um novo apartamento)
11. has – moved (Ele acaba/acabou de mudar)
12. have travel(l)ed (Viajei/tenho viajado de trem muitas vezes)

2. (pág. 61)
1. has – begun
2. have been
3. haven't heard
4. hasn't started
5. didn't go
6. hasn't talked
7. haven't been
8. have eaten
9. Has – been
10. have written
11. bought
12. learned
13. didn't go
14. was
15. have been
16. was
17. has been
18. haven't had
19. has spoken
20. haven't sent

PAST PERFECT

1. (pág. 64)
1. had – worked/Eu nunca tinha trabalhado tanto até fazer parte do banco.
2. had left/Na hora em que nós chegamos todos tinham ido embora.
3. had won/Ela me disse que tinha vencido um campeonato havia muito tempo.
4. had got/Ele comprou o carro após ter conseguido um novo emprego.
5. had been/Eles estiveram em greve por um mês antes de fazer um acordo.

2. (pág. 65)
1. arrived
2. had read
3. had finished
4. had left
5. had been
6. had done
7. hadn't heard
8. didn't have
9. had done
10. had hurt

3. (pág. 66)
1. had gone
2. dressed
3. had begun
4. sat down – rested
5. went – found out
6. had been
7. remembered
8. had asked
9. had finished
10. said

FUTURE PERFECT

1. (pág. 68)
1. Até janeiro próximo, terei recebido meu diploma.
2. Até dezembro próximo, eles terão terminado o curso de inglês.
3. Até voltarmos ao nosso país teremos visitado mais de 20 países.
4. Ele não terá aprendido japonês antes de se mudar para o Japão.
5. Terei preparado um delicioso jantar antes de os convidados chegarem.
6. Amanhã, a esta hora, ela terá chegado em casa.

2. (pág. 69)
1. will have written
2. won't have forgotten
3. will have left
4. will have taken
5. will have eaten
6. will have taught
7. will have been
8. will have stopped
9. will have sold
10. will have bought

3. (pág. 69)
1. will have met your boyfriend.
2. Our daughter will have stayed
3. will have flown more than a million miles.
4. My niece will have grown up
5. I'm sure you will/won't have left
6. will have slept for twenty-four hours.
7. In January he will have been
8. will not have spoken to the pop star.
9. The band will have sung
10. they will have gone to India.

PRESENT / PAST / FUTURE PERFECT PROGRESSIVE

1. (pág. 73)
1. will have been jogging
2. will have been studying
3. has been living
4. will have been watching
5. had been working
6. had been taking
7. have been reading
8. have been looking
9. has been smoking
10. had been trying

2. (pág. 74)
1. I have been trying to finish the letter all morning.
2. They had been asking questions about her before the crime happened.
3. We will have been eating pasta for two weeks tomorrow.
4. He had been watching that picture for hours before talking to us.
5. She has been waiting for the doctor for the last two hours.

CONDITIONAL TENSES

1. (pág. 78)
1. possible
2. improbable
3. improbable
4. improbable
5. impossible
6. improbable
7. possible
8. possible
9. possible
10. impossible
11. impossible
12. impossible
13. possible
14. possible
15. impossible

2. (pág. 79)
1. would feel
2. would have asked
3. would go
4. would get
5. will go
6. would have told
7. will play
8. will get
9. would – keep
10. would go
11. wouldn't have seen
12. should have worked
13. wouldn't have talked
14. won't buy
15. would have publish

3. (pág. 80)
1. would be
2. would have spoken
3. won't get
4. will tell
5. would – do
6. would have understood
7. won't catch
8. would have helped
9. will go
10. would sleep

PRÁTICA ADICIONAL

SIMPLE TENSES

1. (pág. 91)
1. comes
2. takes
3. boils
4. causes
5. asked
6. worked
7. did – buy
8. don't like
9. will go
10. are – going to do

2. (pág. 92)
1. puts
2. will see
3. are – going to do/will – do
4. will ring
5. lost
6. will talk
7. misses
8. read
9. did
10. ate

3 (pág. 92)
1. She bakes a cake everyday.
2. The sun shone in Egypt yesterday.
3. I will wake up at 7:00 and will have breakfast at 7:30 tomorrow.
4. We didn't sleep there because we were not tired.
5. She doesn't open the door because she doesn't know you.

PROGRESSIVE TENSES

1. (pág. 92)
1. is raining
2. is happening/is going on
3. will be having
4. was driving
5. is waiting
6. were playing
7. Will you be working
8. will be waiting
9. was looking
10. were crossing

2. (pág. 94)
1. were preparing
2. will be waiting
3. were – doing
4. was sitting
5. will be watching
6. will be discussing
7. is sleeping
8. are saying/is talking
9. were playing
10. will be driving
11. are flying
12. will be studying
13. was practicing
14. am trying to work
15. aren't listening
16. was coming
17. were doing
18. were having
19. Are – listening
20. Is – writing

PERFECT TENSES

1. (pág. 95)
1. has been
2. had had
3. will have bought
4. have talked
5. will have taught
6. have heard
7. Haven't – taken
8. hadn't helped
9. have read
10. have swum
11. Had – talked
12. will have walked
13. will have been
14. had broken
15. haven't seen

PERFECT PROGRESSIVE TENSES

1. (pág. 96)
1. had been
2. have been
3. have been
4. had been
5. had been
6. will have been
7. will have been
8. has been
9. have been
10. has been

11. *have been*
12. *will have been*
13. *had been*
14. *had been*
15. *had been*

CONDITIONAL TENSES

1. (pág. 97)
1. *I will finish the letter*
2. *they would go to the movies*
3. *I would have come sooner*
4. *she would have talked to you*
5. *We will move to Alagoas*
6. *She will apologize*
7. *I would have sold you the house*
8. *We won't work tomorrow*
9. *he would go away*
10. *I wouldn't be sad*

Verbos Irregulares

Veja a seguir uma lista de verbos irregulares. Alguns verbos têm duas formas em uso – a regular e a irregular.

Base Form	Past Tense	Past Participle	Translation
abide	abode/abided	abode	tolerar
arise	arose	arisen	surgir
awake	awoke	awoken	acordar
be	was/were	been	ser/estar
bear	bore	born	suportar
beat	beat	beaten	bater
become	became	become	tornar-se
begin	began	begun	começar
behold	beheld	beheld	observar
bend	bent	bent	curvar
bet	bet	bet	apostar
bid	bid	bid/bidden	ordenar
bind	bound	bound	atar
bite	bit	bitten	morder
bleed	bled	bled	sangrar
blow	blew	blown	soprar
break	broke	broken	quebrar
breed	bred	bred	criar
bring	brought	brought	trazer
build	built	built	construir
burn	burned/burnt	burned/burnt	queimar
burst	burst	burst	explodir
bust	bust	bust	estourar

Base Form	Past Tense	Past Participle	Translation
buy	bought	bought	comprar
cast	cast	cast	arremessar
catch	caught	caught	pegar
choose	chose	chosen	escolher
clap	clapped	clapped	aplaudir
cling	clung	clung	agarrar
come	came	come	vir
cost	cost	cost	custar
creep	crept	crept	rastejar
cut	cut	cut	cortar
deal	dealt	dealt	tratar
dig	dug	dug	cavar
dive	dived/dove	dived	mergulhar
do	did	done	fazer
draw	drew	drawn	desenhar
dream	dreamed/dreamt	dreamed/dreamt	sonhar
drink	drank	drunk	beber
dwell	dwelled/dwelt	dwelled/dwelt	habitar
eat	ate	eaten	comer
fall	fell	fallen	cair
feed	fed	fed	alimentar
feel	felt	felt	sentir
fight	fought	fought	lutar
find	found	found	achar
fit	fitted/fit	fitted/fit	adaptar
flee	fled	fled	fugir
fling	flung	flung	arremessar
fly	flew	flown	voar
forbid	forbade	forbidden	proibir
forget	forgot	forgotten	esquecer
freeze	froze	frozen	congelar
get	got	got/gotten	conseguir
give	gave	given	dar

Base Form	Past Tense	Past Participle	Translation
go	went	gone	ir
grind	ground	ground	moer
grow	grew	grown	crescer
hang	hung	hung	pendurar
have	had	had	ter
hear	heard	heard	ouvir
hide	hid	hid/hidden	esconder
hit	hit	hit	bater
hold	held	held	segurar
hurt	hurt	hurt	ferir
keep	kept	kept	manter
kneel	kneeled/knelt	kneeled/knelt	ajoelhar-se
knit	knitted/knit	knitted/knit	tricotar
know	knew	known	saber
lay	laid	laid	pôr
lead	led	led	conduzir
lean	leaned/leant	leaned/leant	inclinar
leap	leapt	leapt	pular
learn	learned/learnt	learned/learnt	aprender
leave	left	left	sair
lend	lent	lent	emprestar
let	let	let	deixar
lie	lay	lain	deitar-se; situar
light	lighted/lit	lighted/lit	acender
lose	lost	lost	perder
make	made	made	fazer
mean	meant	meant	significar
meet	met	met	encontrar
mow	mowed	mowed/mown	aparar
pay	paid	paid	pagar
put	put	put	pôr
quit	quitted/quit	quitted/quit	desistir
read	read	read	ler

Base Form	Past Tense	Past Participle	Translation
rid	ridded/rid	ridded/rid	libertar(-se)
ride	rode	ridden	andar de
ring	rang	rung	tocar; soar
rise	rose	risen	levantar-se
rive	rived	rived/riven	rachar
run	ran	run	correr
saw	sawed	sawed/sawn	serrar
say	said	said	dizer
see	saw	seen	ver
seek	sought	sought	procurar
sell	sold	sold	vender
send	sent	sent	enviar
set	set	set	pôr
sew	sewed	sewed/sewn	costurar
shake	shook	shaken	agitar
shear	sheared/shore	sheared/shorn	tosar
shed	shed	shed	abrigar
shine	shone	shone	brilhar
shoe	shod	shod/shodden	calçar
shoot	shot	shot	atirar
show	showed	showed/shown	mostrar; exibir
shrink	shrank	shrunk	encolher
shut	shut	shut	fechar
sing	sang	sung	cantar
sink	sank	sunk	afundar
sit	sat	sat	sentar
slay	slew	slain	assassinar
sleep	slept	slept	dormir
slide	slid	slid	deslizar
sling	slung	slung	lançar
slink	slunk/slinked	slunk/slinked	esquivar-se
slit	slit	slit	rachar
smell	smelled/smelt	smelled/smelt	cheirar

Base Form	Past Tense	Past Participle	Translation
sneak	sneaked/snuck	sneaked/snuck	andar furtivamente
sow	sowed	sowed/sown	semear
speak	spoke	spoken	falar
speed	speeded/sped	speeded/sped	correr
spell	spelled/spelt	spelled/spelt	soletrar
spend	spent	spent	gastar
spill	spilled/spilt	spilled/spilt	derramar
spin	span	spun	fiar; girar
spit	spit/spat	spit/spat	cuspir
slit	split	split	dividir
spoil	spoiled/spoit	spoiled/spoilt	estragar
spread	spread	spread	espalhar
spring	sprang	sprung	saltar
stand	stood	stood	permanecer
steal	stole	stolen	roubar
stick	stuck	stuck	grudar
sting	stung	stung	picar
stink	stank	stunk	cheirar mal
stride	strode	stridden	andar com passadas largas
strike	struck	struck	golpear
string	strung	strung	enfileirar; amarrar
strip	stripped/strip	stripped/strip	desnudar
strive	strove/strived	striven/strived	esforçar-se; lutar
swear	swore	sworn	jurar
sweat	sweated/sweat	sweated/sweat	transpirar
sweep	swept	swept	varrer
swell	swelled	swelled/swollen	inchar; intensificar
swim	swam	swum	nadar
swing	swung	swung	balançar

Base Form	Past Tense	Past Participle	Translation
take	took	taken	tomar
teach	taught	taught	ensinar
tear	tore	torn	rasgar
tell	told	told	contar
think	thought	thought	pensar
thrive	thrived/throve	thrived/thriven	prosperar; desenvolver-se
throw	threw	thrown	atirar
thrust	thrust	thrust	impelir
tread	trod	trodden	marchar
undergo	underwent	undergone	aguentar
understand	understood	understood	entender
upset	upset	upset	tombar; perturbar
vex	vexed	vexed	atormentar
wake	waked/woke	waked/woken	acordar
wear	wore	worn	vestir
weave	wove	woven	tecer
wed	wed	wed	casar(-se)
weep	wept	wept	chorar
wend	wended	wended	dirigir-se para
wet	wetted/wet	wetted/wet	molhar
win	won	won	vencer
wind	wound	wound	dar corda
withdraw	withdrew	withdrawn	retrair
withhold	withheld	withheld	reter
withstand	withstood	withstood	resistir; opor-se
wring	wrung	wrung	torcer(-se)
write	wrote	written	escrever

Este livro foi composto nas fontes Stag e Mercury e
impresso em março de 2024 pela Paym Gráfica Editora Ltda.,
sobre papel offset 75g/m².